Throughout this book, you'll learn about frameworks that have been used by successful individuals and organizations across different fields and industries. These frameworks have been tried and tested, and have proven to be effective in helping people achieve their goals and reach their full potential.

By using the frameworks in this book, you'll be able to:

Set and achieve goals that align with your values and aspirations
Prioritize your tasks and focus on what's most important
Manage your time more effectively and efficiently
Identify and overcome obstacles and challenges
Cultivate a growth mindset and embrace new opportunities for learning and development
Make better decisions more quickly and confidently
Build competence and expertise in your chosen field or area of interest
Cultivate positive habits and behaviors that support your success

Avoid common traps and pitfalls that can derail your progress

Whether you're just starting out on your path to success, or you're looking to take your achievements to the next level, the frameworks in this book can help you get there. With practical tools and resources that you can use to apply each framework to your own goals and situations, you'll be able to make progress more quickly and efficiently than you ever thought possible.

So let's dive in and discover how frameworks can help you achieve your goals and become more successful in all areas of your life!

Introduction: Why Frameworks are a Shortcut to Success

Do you ever feel like achieving your goals is an overwhelming and daunting task? Do you struggle to stay motivated and focused on your path to success? If so, you're not alone. Many people struggle with achieving their goals and making meaningful progress towards success.

The good news is that there is a solution: frameworks. Frameworks are proven strategies and systems that can help you achieve your goals more efficiently and effectively. By using frameworks, you can take a shortcut to success by leveraging the experiences and insights of others who have achieved success in their own lives.

In this book, you'll learn about 15 frameworks that can help you achieve your goals and become more successful in all areas of your life. From SMART goals to the Pareto Principle to the Growth Mindset, each framework is designed to help you maximize your effectiveness and achieve your goals with less effort and greater efficiency.

But why are frameworks so effective? The answer lies in their ability to provide structure and direction to your efforts. Rather than trying to reinvent the wheel or navigate the complex landscape of success on your own, frameworks provide a roadmap that you can follow to achieve your goals. By using frameworks, you can avoid common pitfalls and mistakes, make progress more quickly, and stay motivated and focused on your path to success.

In the chapters that follow, you'll learn about each framework in detail, including how to apply it to your own life and goals. You'll also find practical resources and tools that you can use to put each framework into practice, including worksheets, checklists, and reflection exercises.

Whether you're looking to achieve success in your career, relationships, health, or personal development, the frameworks in this book can help you get there faster and more efficiently. So let's get started and discover how frameworks can be a shortcut to success!

Chapter 1: Setting SMART Goals

Do you ever feel like you're spinning your wheels, working hard but not making meaningful progress towards your goals? Or maybe you struggle to define and achieve your goals in the first place? If so, you're not alone. Many people struggle with goal-setting and achieving their desired outcomes.

The good news is that there is a solution: SMART Goals. SMART stands for specific, measurable, achievable, relevant, and time-bound. This framework provides a clear and effective way to set and achieve goals that are well-defined, realistic, and focused on your desired outcomes.

In this book, you'll learn how to use the SMART Goals framework to achieve success in all areas of your life. Whether you're looking to advance in your career, improve your health, build better relationships, or pursue personal growth, the SMART framework can help you get there faster and more efficiently.

Each element of SMART Goals is designed to help you create goals that are clear, actionable, and focused on your desired outcomes. By setting goals that are specific, measurable, achievable, relevant, and time-bound, you can make meaningful progress towards success and achieve your most important goals.

But why are SMART Goals so effective? The answer lies in their ability to provide structure and direction to your efforts. Rather than setting vague or ambiguous goals, SMART Goals provide a clear roadmap that you can follow to achieve your desired outcomes. This makes it easier to stay motivated, focused, and accountable, and to make progress more quickly and efficiently than you ever thought possible.

In the following chapters, you'll learn about each element of the SMART Goals framework in detail, including how to apply it to your own goals and situations. You'll also find practical resources and tools that you can use to put the SMART framework into practice, including worksheets, checklists, and reflection exercises.

So let's get started and discover the power of SMART Goals!

The Five Elements of SMART Goals

Setting SMART Goals involves five essential elements that work together to create clear, actionable goals. Let's take a closer look at each element:

Specific: The first element of SMART Goals is specificity. A specific goal is well-defined and clear, so you know exactly what you're working towards. To make your goals specific, use the 5 Ws: who, what, where, when, and why. This will help you create a goal statement that is focused and actionable. For example, instead of setting a goal to "get in shape," a more specific goal could be "lose 10 pounds in 3 months by exercising for 30 minutes a day and following a healthy eating plan."

Measurable: The second element of SMART Goals is measurability. A measurable goal is one that you can track your progress towards and determine whether or not you've achieved it. This could be a number, a percentage, or a specific outcome. For example, if your goal is to increase your sales, you could set a measurable goal of "increase sales by 20% in the next quarter."

Achievable: The third element of SMART Goals is achievability. An achievable goal is one that is realistic and attainable given your resources, abilities, and constraints. While it's important to challenge yourself, it's also important to set goals that are within your reach. For example, if you're just starting out with exercise, it may be unrealistic to set a goal of running a marathon in a month.

Relevant: The fourth element of SMART Goals is relevance. A relevant goal is one that aligns with your values, aspirations, and long-term objectives. It should be meaningful and important to you, rather than something that others expect of you. For example, if your goal is to become a successful entrepreneur, it should be relevant to your interests and skills.

Time-bound: The fifth and final element of SMART Goals is time-bound. A time-bound goal has a specific deadline or timeline attached to it. This creates a sense of urgency and helps you stay on track towards achieving your goal. For example, if your goal is to write a book, you should set a deadline for when you want to complete it.

By incorporating each of these elements into your goal-setting process, you can create goals that are clear, actionable, and focused on your desired outcomes. This will help you make meaningful progress towards success and achieve your most important goals.

Benefits of SMART Goals

Setting goals is essential for achieving success in any area of life, but not all goals are created equal. By using the SMART Goals framework, you can reap numerous benefits that can help you achieve your goals more effectively. Let's take a closer look at some of the key benefits of using SMART Goals:

Increased Focus: SMART Goals provide a clear and well-defined roadmap for achieving your desired outcomes. By setting specific and measurable goals, you can focus your efforts on the most important tasks and avoid getting distracted by less important activities. This helps you stay on track towards achieving your goals and makes it easier to stay motivated and focused.

Motivation: SMART Goals help to create a sense of purpose and motivation by providing a clear target to work towards. When you have a specific and achievable goal in mind, you are more likely to feel energized and motivated to take action. This can help you overcome obstacles and stay committed to your goals over the long-term.

Accountability: SMART Goals help to create a sense of accountability by setting clear expectations for what you want to achieve and by when. By setting a specific deadline or timeline for achieving your goals, you are more likely to stay on track and avoid procrastination. Additionally, by tracking your progress towards your goals, you can hold yourself accountable and make adjustments as needed.

Improved Decision-making: SMART Goals provide a framework for making better decisions by helping you focus on what is most important. When you have a specific and measurable goal in mind, you can evaluate different options and choose the one that is most likely to help you achieve your desired outcome.

Increased Self-confidence: By achieving your SMART Goals, you can build a sense of self-confidence and self-efficacy. When you set realistic and achievable goals, and then follow through with them, you build a track record of success that can help you tackle even bigger challenges in the future.

Overall, the benefits of SMART Goals are numerous and far-reaching. By using this framework, you can create goals that are clear, actionable, and focused on your desired outcomes, and make meaningful progress towards achieving your most important goals.

Common Mistakes to Avoid

While setting goals can be a powerful way to achieve success, there are also common mistakes that people make that can prevent them from reaching their desired outcomes. Let's take a look at some of these common mistakes and how the SMART Goals framework can help you avoid them:

Vague or Ambiguous Goals: One common mistake is setting goals that are too vague or ambiguous. For example, setting a goal to "be more successful" is not specific enough to provide a clear roadmap for success. By using the SMART Goals framework, you can make your goals more specific, measurable, and well-defined, so you know exactly what you're working towards.

Unrealistic Goals: Another common mistake is setting goals that are unrealistic or unattainable given your resources, abilities, and constraints. By using the achievability element of SMART Goals, you can set goals that are challenging yet achievable, and avoid setting yourself up for failure.

Lack of Relevance: Setting goals that are not relevant to your values, aspirations, and long-term objectives is another common mistake. By using the relevance element of SMART Goals, you can ensure that your goals align with your priorities and interests, and are meaningful and important to you.

Lack of Accountability: Setting goals without a clear deadline or timeline for achieving them can lead to procrastination and lack of accountability. By using the time-bound element of SMART Goals, you can create a sense of urgency and hold yourself accountable for achieving your goals.

Failure to Track Progress: Finally, failing to track your progress towards your goals can prevent you from making meaningful progress and staying motivated. By using the measurable element of SMART Goals, you can track your progress and make adjustments as needed to ensure that you are on track towards achieving your desired outcomes.

Now that you understand the five elements of SMART Goals and the benefits of using this framework, let's take a closer look at how you can apply it to goal-setting in different areas of life:

Career Goals: If you're looking to advance in your career, use the SMART Goals framework to set specific, measurable, and achievable goals that are relevant to your desired outcomes. For example, if you want to get promoted to a higher position, set a SMART goal to increase your performance metrics by a specific percentage over the next six months.

Health Goals: If you're looking to improve your health, use the SMART Goals framework to set specific and achievable goals that are relevant to your health goals. For example, if you want to lose weight, set a SMART goal to lose a specific number of pounds over the next three months by following a healthy eating plan and exercising for a specific amount of time each week.

Relationship Goals: If you're looking to improve your relationships, use the SMART Goals framework to set specific and relevant goals that focus on building stronger connections with your loved ones. For example, if you want to improve your communication with your partner, set a SMART goal to have regular date nights and meaningful conversations each week.

Personal Development Goals: If you're looking to pursue personal growth and development, use the SMART Goals framework to set specific and achievable goals that are relevant to your desired outcomes. For example, if you want to improve your public speaking skills, set a SMART goal to attend a public speaking course and practice your skills in front of others at least once a week.

When applying the SMART Goals framework to different areas of life, it's important to keep in mind that each area may require different types of goals and different levels of specificity and achievability. Use the framework to create goals that are relevant to your desired outcomes, and adjust them as needed to ensure that they are achievable and well-defined.

In addition to setting SMART Goals, it's also important to track your progress and make adjustments as needed. Regularly reviewing your goals and tracking your progress towards achieving them can help you stay motivated and make meaningful progress towards success.

By applying the SMART Goals framework to different areas of your life, you can create clear and actionable goals that are focused on your desired outcomes. This will help you achieve success and make meaningful progress towards your most important goals.

The SMART Goals framework has been used by individuals and organizations across various industries and sectors to achieve their goals and make meaningful progress towards success. Let's take a look at some real-life examples of how the SMART Goals framework has been applied in practice:

In 2014, Microsoft implemented the SMART Goals framework as part of its "One Microsoft" initiative, which aimed to increase employee engagement, productivity, and overall performance. The framework was used to help employees set and achieve their goals, with a focus on creating goals that were specific, measurable, achievable, relevant, and time-bound.

By using the SMART Goals framework, Microsoft employees were able to create goals that were well-defined and actionable, with clear metrics for success. They were able to track their progress towards these goals and make adjustments as needed to ensure that they stayed on track.

One of the key benefits of using the SMART Goals framework at Microsoft was increased employee engagement and motivation. By giving employees a clear roadmap for success and providing them with the tools to track their progress, employees felt more empowered and accountable for achieving their goals. This led to increased productivity, as employees were more focused and motivated to perform at their best.

In addition to increased engagement and productivity, Microsoft also saw improvements in overall performance as a result of using the SMART Goals framework. By aligning individual goals with the company's overall objectives, employees were better able to contribute to the company's success and achieve meaningful results.

SMART GOALS

S SPECIFIC

M MEASURABLE

A ACHIEVABLE

R RELEVANT

T TIME BOUND

Chapter 2: Prioritize With The Eisenhower Matrix

Do you ever feel overwhelmed by your to-do list, unsure of where to start or how to prioritize tasks? If so, you're not alone. Many people struggle with effective time management and productivity, especially in today's fast-paced and constantly changing world.

One framework that can help with this challenge is the Eisenhower Matrix. This framework, named after former US President Dwight D. Eisenhower, is a tool for prioritizing tasks based on their importance and urgency. By using the Eisenhower Matrix, you can better manage your time and focus on the tasks that are most important for achieving your goals.

The concept of the Eisenhower Matrix is simple but powerful. The matrix is divided into four quadrants, each representing a different combination of importance and urgency. Tasks are categorized into one of these quadrants, based on their level of importance and urgency, and then prioritized accordingly.

The benefits of using the Eisenhower Matrix for effective time management and productivity are significant. By prioritizing tasks based on their importance and urgency, you can focus on the tasks that are most critical for achieving your goals, while also managing your time more efficiently. This can lead to increased productivity, reduced stress, and a greater sense of accomplishment.

In this chapter, we will explore the concept of the Eisenhower Matrix in more detail, including how it works, how to apply it in different settings, and the benefits of using this framework for effective time management and productivity. We will also provide practical tips and strategies for using the Eisenhower Matrix in your own life, and share real-life examples of individuals and organizations who have successfully applied this framework to achieve their goals.

The Eisenhower Matrix is divided into four quadrants, each representing a different combination of importance and urgency:

Important and Urgent: This quadrant represents tasks that are both important and urgent, and require immediate attention. These tasks are often critical for achieving your goals or preventing negative consequences. Examples of tasks that might fall into this quadrant include deadlines, emergencies, and crises.

Important but Not Urgent: This quadrant represents tasks that are important but not urgent, and require proactive planning and prioritization. These tasks are often critical for achieving your long-term goals or improving your overall quality of life. Examples of tasks that might fall into this quadrant include long-term planning, relationship building, and skill development.

Urgent but Not Important: This quadrant represents tasks that are urgent but not important, and can often be a distraction from more critical tasks. These tasks may be time-sensitive, but do not contribute significantly to your goals or overall well-being. Examples of tasks that might fall into this quadrant include interruptions, meetings, and emails.

Not Important and Not Urgent: This quadrant represents tasks that are neither important nor urgent, and can often be eliminated or delegated. These tasks may be time-wasters or low-priority activities that do not contribute significantly to your goals or overall well-being. Examples of tasks that might fall into this quadrant include browsing social media, watching TV, or running errands.

It's important to distinguish between important and urgent tasks, as this can help you prioritize your to-do list and focus on the tasks that are most critical for achieving your goals. Urgent tasks may require immediate attention, but if they are not important, they can be a distraction from more critical tasks. On the other hand, important tasks may not be urgent, but they are critical for achieving your long-term goals and improving your overall well-being.

By categorizing tasks into the four quadrants of the Eisenhower Matrix, you can better prioritize your to-do list and focus on the tasks that are most critical for achieving your goals. This can lead to increased productivity, reduced stress, and a greater sense of accomplishment.

Now that you understand the four quadrants of the Eisenhower Matrix and how they relate to the concepts of importance and urgency, let's explore some practical tips and strategies for using this framework to prioritize tasks and manage time effectively.

Start by identifying all of your tasks: To effectively use the Eisenhower Matrix, you need to start by identifying all of the tasks that are on your to-do list. Write down everything that you need to accomplish, no matter how big or small.

Categorize tasks into the four quadrants: Once you have identified all of your tasks, it's time to categorize them into the four quadrants of the Eisenhower Matrix. Be honest with yourself about the level of importance and urgency of each task, and categorize them accordingly.

Prioritize tasks within each quadrant: Once you have categorized your tasks, it's time to prioritize them within each quadrant. Identify the most critical tasks within each quadrant and focus on those first. This will ensure that you are spending your time on the tasks that are most important for achieving your goals.

Regularly review and update the matrix: The Eisenhower Matrix is not a one-time exercise. It's important to regularly review and update the matrix to ensure that tasks are properly categorized and prioritized. This will help you stay focused on your goals and make adjustments as needed.

Use the Eisenhower Matrix in different settings: The Eisenhower Matrix can be used in a variety of settings, including at work and in personal life. For example, you can use the matrix to prioritize tasks within a project, or to prioritize personal tasks such as exercise and self-care.

At work: Let's say you're working on a project with a tight deadline. You have several tasks to complete, including conducting research, creating a presentation, and coordinating with team members. By using the Eisenhower Matrix, you can categorize these tasks based on their importance and urgency. For example, you might categorize the research and presentation creation as important and urgent, and the coordination with team members as important but not urgent.

With this information, you can focus your attention on completing the important and urgent tasks first, ensuring that you meet the project deadline. You can then schedule time for the important but not urgent tasks, such as coordinating with team members, to ensure that you are making progress on the project without sacrificing the urgent tasks.

In addition, the Eisenhower Matrix can help you prioritize tasks across different projects. Let's say you have multiple projects with different deadlines and priorities. By categorizing each task in the matrix, you can identify the tasks that are most critical for each project and ensure that you are making progress on all of your projects without getting overwhelmed.

In personal life: Let's say you're a busy parent with a full-time job and other personal responsibilities. By using the Eisenhower Matrix, you can prioritize your tasks and ensure that you are making time for the things that are most important to you.

For example, you might categorize spending time with family and exercising as important but not urgent, and attending work meetings and completing household chores as urgent but not important. With this information, you can schedule regular time for family activities and exercise, ensuring that you prioritize your health and well-being. You can also delegate household chores to other family members or hire a cleaning service, freeing up more time for the important but not urgent tasks.

In addition, the Eisenhower Matrix can help you prioritize personal development activities, such as reading or taking courses. By categorizing these activities as important but not urgent, you can schedule regular time for them and ensure that you are making progress on your personal goals.

Overall, the Eisenhower Matrix is a powerful tool for managing your time and achieving your goals, both at work and in your personal life. By using real-life examples, we can see how this framework can be applied in various settings to achieve greater productivity and success.

Common Challenges and Solutions

While the Eisenhower Matrix can be an effective tool for managing time and prioritizing tasks, there are several common challenges that people may face when using this framework. In this section, we will discuss these challenges and provide solutions for overcoming them.

Difficulty distinguishing between important and urgent tasks: One of the most common challenges people face when using the Eisenhower Matrix is accurately categorizing tasks based on their importance and urgency. This can be particularly challenging when tasks are time-sensitive, or when there are multiple tasks vying for your attention.
Solution: To overcome this challenge, it can be helpful to set clear criteria for what constitutes important and urgent tasks. For example, you might define an important task as one that contributes to your long-term goals or has a significant impact on your overall well-being, while an urgent task is one that requires immediate attention to avoid negative consequences.

Overestimating the urgency of certain tasks: Another common challenge people face when using the Eisenhower Matrix is overestimating the urgency of certain tasks. This can lead to spending too much time on tasks that are not actually urgent, or neglecting tasks that are important but not urgent.

Solution: To overcome this challenge, it can be helpful to take a step back and objectively evaluate each task based on its actual urgency. This might involve asking questions such as "What would happen if I didn't complete this task right away?" or "What are the consequences of delaying this task?" By gaining a clearer understanding of the true urgency of each task, you can prioritize your time and attention more effectively.

Feeling overwhelmed by a large number of tasks: Finally, another common challenge people face when using the Eisenhower Matrix is feeling overwhelmed by a large number of tasks. This can lead to procrastination or indecision, as it can be difficult to know where to start.

Solution: To overcome this challenge, it can be helpful to break down large tasks into smaller, more manageable steps. You might also consider delegating tasks that are not important or urgent, or seeking help from others when necessary. By breaking down large tasks and focusing on one step at a time, you can make progress without feeling overwhelmed.

Overall, while the Eisenhower Matrix can be a powerful tool for managing time and prioritizing tasks, it is important to be aware of common challenges and strategies for overcoming them. By setting clear criteria for importance and urgency, objectively evaluating each task, and breaking down large tasks into smaller steps, you can effectively apply the Eisenhower Matrix and achieve greater productivity and success.

In this section, we will share real-life examples of individuals or organizations who have successfully used the Eisenhower Matrix to prioritize tasks and achieve their goals. By examining these case studies, we can gain insights into the specific strategies and techniques that were used and how they can be applied to other situations.

Elon Musk is one of the most successful entrepreneurs of our time, known for his ambitious goals and busy schedule. He has been the CEO of multiple companies, including Tesla, SpaceX, Neuralink, and The Boring

Company. To manage his time effectively, Musk uses the Eisenhower Matrix to prioritize his tasks and ensure that he is focusing on the most important and urgent tasks first.

One specific strategy that Musk uses is to break down large tasks into smaller, more manageable steps. For example, when SpaceX was working on its first rocket launch, Musk divided the task into smaller steps, such as testing the engines, building the launch pad, and conducting a test flight. By breaking down the task in this way, he could more easily identify the most important and urgent steps and ensure that progress was being made.

Musk also delegates tasks that are not important or urgent to others, freeing up more time for the tasks that require his attention. For example, he has delegated day-to-day operations of SpaceX to other executives, allowing him to focus on the company's long-term strategy and vision.

In addition to using the Eisenhower Matrix himself, Musk also encourages his staff to use the framework in their own work. By aligning everyone on priorities, the team can work more efficiently and effectively towards common goals.

Google is a company that is known for its innovative products and fast-paced work environment. To manage this environment effectively, Google uses the Eisenhower Matrix to prioritize tasks and ensure that employees are focusing on the most important and urgent tasks.

One specific strategy that Google uses is to encourage employees to set clear goals and align them with the company's overall mission and objectives. This ensures that employees are working on tasks that are aligned with the company's priorities and are contributing to its overall success. For example, Google's "OKR" (Objectives and Key Results) system sets company-wide goals and helps employees understand how their individual goals contribute to the bigger picture.

Google also encourages employees to collaborate and delegate tasks to others when necessary, ensuring that everyone is working together to achieve common goals. This helps to prevent individuals from becoming overwhelmed with too many tasks and allows for more efficient use of resources.

Additionally, Google regularly reviews and updates the Eisenhower Matrix to ensure that tasks are properly categorized and prioritized. The company understands that priorities can shift quickly, especially in a fast-paced environment, so regularly revisiting the matrix ensures that everyone is up-to-date on priorities and can adjust their work accordingly.

One example of how Google has used the Eisenhower Matrix to improve productivity is by implementing a program called "Gmail Zero." This program encourages employees to aim for an empty inbox by the end of each day, with emails categorized by importance and urgency using the Eisenhower Matrix. By doing this, employees can ensure that they are responding to important and urgent emails first, and can avoid getting bogged down by less important messages.

Overall, the case of Google demonstrates how the Eisenhower Matrix can be an effective tool for managing time and prioritizing tasks in a fast-paced and constantly changing environment. By encouraging clear goals, collaboration, and regular updates to the matrix, Google has been able to achieve incredible success and maintain its position as a leader in the tech industry.

In conclusion, the Eisenhower Matrix is a powerful framework that can help individuals and organizations prioritize tasks and manage time more effectively. By distinguishing between tasks that are important and urgent, and regularly reviewing and updating the matrix, individuals can ensure that they are focusing on the most important tasks first and avoiding distractions that can derail productivity.

The benefits of using the Eisenhower Matrix include increased productivity, greater focus, and improved decision-making. By using the matrix, individuals can better allocate their time and resources towards achieving their goals and fulfilling their responsibilities.

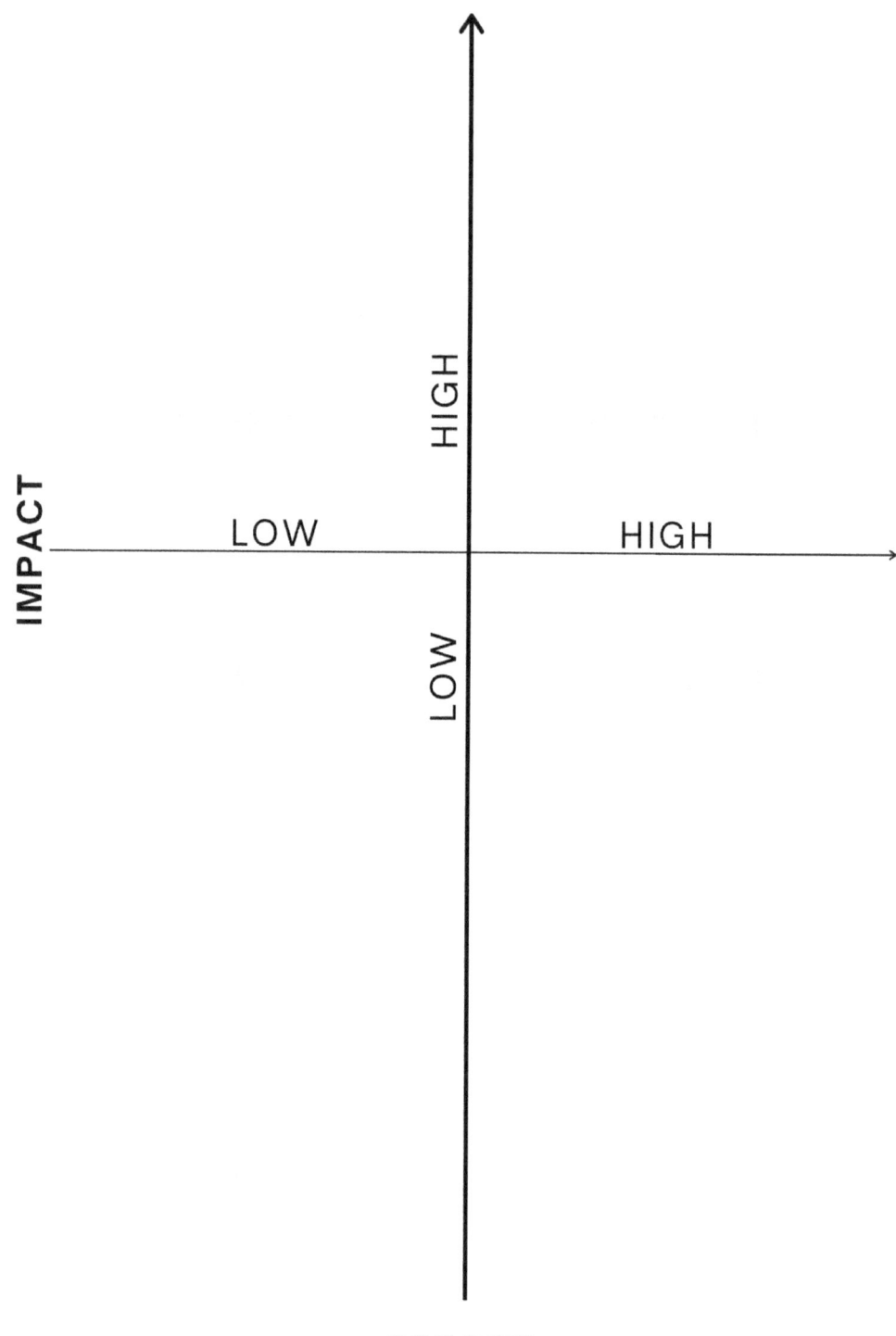

Chapter 3: Time Management Using The Pomodoro Technique

The Pomodoro Technique is a time-management framework that has gained popularity in recent years as a way to improve productivity and focus. The technique involves breaking work into manageable intervals, typically 25 minutes long, separated by short breaks. This method is designed to help individuals work more efficiently by focusing on one task at a time and taking frequent breaks to avoid burnout.

The Pomodoro Technique was developed in the late 1980s by Francesco Cirillo, a software developer who was struggling with procrastination and distraction. He developed the technique as a way to manage his time more effectively and improve his focus. The name "pomodoro" is Italian for "tomato," and was inspired by the tomato-shaped kitchen timer that Cirillo used to time his work intervals.

There are several benefits to using the Pomodoro Technique. One of the main benefits is improved time management, as the technique helps individuals prioritize tasks and focus on one task at a time. This can also help reduce procrastination and increase motivation, as individuals are able to break larger tasks into smaller, more manageable parts. In addition, taking frequent breaks can help reduce stress and fatigue, which can ultimately improve overall productivity.

Overall, the Pomodoro Technique is a powerful tool for anyone looking to improve their time management skills and increase their productivity. In the following sections, we will explore how the technique works, how to overcome common challenges, and practical tips and strategies for applying the technique in various settings.

The Pomodoro Technique is a simple but powerful time-management framework that can help individuals break down tasks into manageable intervals, and stay focused and productive throughout the day. The basic structure of the technique is as follows:

Set a timer for 25 minutes: The first step in the Pomodoro Technique is to set a timer for 25 minutes. This time interval is called a "pomodoro" (Italian for "tomato"), and is the standard length for each work interval.

Work on a task for 25 minutes: Once the timer is set, the individual should work on a specific task for the entire 25 minutes without any distractions. This means turning off notifications, closing unnecessary tabs, and focusing solely on the task at hand.

Take a short break: After the 25 minutes are up, the individual should take a short break of 5 minutes. This break is designed to help the individual relax and recharge before starting the next pomodoro.

Repeat the process: Once the break is over, the individual should start another 25-minute pomodoro and continue to work on the task. After four pomodoros, the individual should take a longer break of 15-30 minutes before starting the process over again.

The Pomodoro Technique can be applied to a variety of different types of work, including writing, studying, programming, and more. For example, a writer could set a timer for 25 minutes and work on a specific section of their book or article, while a programmer could use the technique to focus on a specific coding task without distractions.

The science behind the Pomodoro Technique is rooted in the concept of "flow," which is a state of deep focus and productivity that occurs when individuals are fully engaged in a task. The technique helps individuals enter a state of flow by breaking down tasks into manageable intervals, which makes it easier to concentrate and reduces the effects of interruptions.

In addition, the Pomodoro Technique can help individuals reduce stress and fatigue by incorporating short breaks into the work process. This can help prevent burnout and improve overall productivity in the long run.

The Pomodoro Technique can be applied to a variety of different areas of life, including work, school, or personal projects. In this section, we will provide practical tips and strategies for applying the technique to different types of work, and discuss how to integrate it into a daily routine.

Apply the technique to different types of work: The Pomodoro Technique can be applied to a variety of different types of work, including writing, studying, or coding. When using the technique, it's important to adjust the length of the pomodoros based on the type of task. For example, a complex coding task may require longer pomodoros, while a simpler task may require shorter intervals. Additionally, it's important to take breaks between pomodoros to allow the brain to recharge and prevent burnout.

Integrate the technique into a daily routine: The Pomodoro Technique can be easily integrated into a daily routine by setting aside specific times of the day for focused work. For example, an individual may set aside two hours in the morning for focused work using the technique, and then take a break before starting the next session. It's important to be consistent and make the technique a habit, as this will increase its effectiveness over time.

Adjust the technique for different settings: The Pomodoro Technique can be adjusted for different settings, such as in education or business. For example, a teacher may use the technique to help students focus during a test or exam, while a business professional may use it to improve productivity during meetings or brainstorming sessions. It's important to be flexible and adapt the technique to fit the specific needs of the setting.

Examples of successful use of the technique: The Pomodoro Technique has been successfully used in a variety of different settings, including education and business. For example, a study conducted at the University of British Columbia found that using the technique helped students improve their focus and retention during study sessions. In business, companies such as Dropbox and BuzzFeed have implemented the technique to improve productivity and reduce burnout among employees.

While the Pomodoro Technique is a powerful tool for time management and productivity on its own, there are many advanced techniques and tools that can be used in combination with it to further enhance its effectiveness.

Task lists: In addition to using the Pomodoro Technique, individuals can also benefit from creating a task list or to-do list. By breaking down larger tasks into smaller, more manageable steps, individuals can better prioritize their work and make progress towards their goals. Additionally, a task list can help individuals stay focused during each pomodoro interval, as they know exactly what needs to be done in the given time frame.

Time tracking software: There are many time tracking software applications available that can be used in conjunction with the Pomodoro Technique. These tools allow individuals to track their progress over time and analyze their work habits, such as how much time is spent on each task or how many pomodoros are completed in a day. This information can be used to identify areas for improvement and optimize the Pomodoro Technique for maximum effectiveness.

Mindfulness practices: Mindfulness practices, such as meditation or breathing exercises, can be used to further enhance the effectiveness of the Pomodoro Technique. By taking a few minutes to clear the mind and focus on the present moment before starting a pomodoro interval, individuals can improve their focus and reduce distractions. Additionally, incorporating mindfulness practices into breaks between pomodoros can help reduce stress and increase overall well-being.

In conclusion, the Pomodoro Technique is a time-management framework that can help individuals improve their productivity and focus by breaking work into manageable intervals. By using a timer and alternating work periods with short breaks, individuals can maintain focus and avoid distractions, leading to increased efficiency and reduced procrastination. Additionally, the technique can help individuals manage their time more effectively, allowing them to balance work and other responsibilities. The Pomodoro Technique is a flexible framework that can be applied to a variety of contexts, from academic and professional work to personal projects and hobbies. By using the Pomodoro Technique in combination with other tools and techniques, individuals can enhance their productivity and achieve their goals more efficiently.

Chapter 4: Maximum Results, Minimal Effort The Pareto Principle:

Introduction:

The Pareto Principle, also known as the 80/20 rule, is a concept that was originally introduced by Italian economist Vilfredo Pareto. In the late 19th century, Pareto observed that 80% of the land in Italy was owned by just 20% of the population. He also noticed that this pattern of unequal distribution occurred in many other areas of life, such as wealth, income, and business.

Based on his observations, Pareto developed the idea that 80% of results come from 20% of causes. This means that a minority of inputs or efforts often account for the majority of outcomes or effects. The Pareto Principle has since been applied in a wide range of fields, including business, economics, engineering, and psychology, to help identify the most impactful actions or investments.

By understanding and applying the Pareto Principle, individuals and organizations can optimize their productivity and efficiency by focusing on the most important tasks or activities that yield the greatest results. This chapter will explore the key concepts and benefits of the Pareto Principle, as well as provide practical tips for applying it in different areas of life.

To understand the Pareto Principle more deeply, it's helpful to look at some examples. In a business context, the principle might suggest that 80% of a company's profits come from 20% of its customers. In personal finance, it could mean that 80% of your expenses come from 20% of your purchases. In time management, it might mean that 80% of your results come from 20% of your efforts.

While the Pareto Principle has been widely applied and accepted, it's not without its limitations and criticisms. Some have argued that the ratios aren't always precisely 80/20, and that the principle oversimplifies complex systems and phenomena. Others have suggested that the principle can be misused or misinterpreted, leading to misguided or overly simplistic decision-making.

The Pareto Principle can be applied to various areas of life for optimizing productivity and efficiency. Here are some practical tips and strategies for applying the Pareto Principle:

Identify the vital few: The first step in applying the Pareto Principle is to identify the 20% of causes that lead to 80% of results. This can be done by analyzing data or by using intuition and experience. Once you identify the vital few, you can prioritize them and focus your efforts on them.

Prioritize tasks: After identifying the vital few, prioritize your tasks accordingly. Focus on completing the tasks that will have the most impact on achieving your goals or completing a project. This will help you to use your time and resources more efficiently.

Simplify: The Pareto Principle can also be applied to simplify your life. Identify the 20% of activities that are taking up 80% of your time and energy, and consider eliminating or delegating them. This can help you to focus on the activities that bring you the most joy and fulfillment.

Evaluate options: When faced with multiple options or decisions, use the Pareto Principle to evaluate the potential outcomes. Consider the 20% of options that will lead to 80% of the desired results and focus on those. This can help you to make better decisions and avoid wasting time and resources on less important options.

Monitor progress: Once you have identified the vital few and prioritized tasks, monitor your progress regularly. This will help you to stay on track and make adjustments as needed. You can also use the Pareto Principle to identify areas where you need to improve and focus your efforts on those areas.

Examples of how the Pareto Principle has been successfully applied include:

In business, the Pareto Principle can be applied to various aspects such as customer base, products or services, and marketing efforts. By focusing on the top 20% of customers that generate 80% of revenue, businesses can prioritize their efforts on retaining those customers and providing them with a premium experience. This can lead to increased customer loyalty and revenue growth.

Similarly, focusing on the top 20% of products that generate 80% of profits can help businesses streamline their product offerings and allocate resources more efficiently. By identifying and prioritizing these products, businesses can focus on improving their quality, marketing them more effectively, and maximizing profits.

In terms of marketing efforts, the Pareto Principle suggests that 80% of a company's sales come from 20% of its marketing campaigns. By identifying the most effective marketing strategies and campaigns, businesses can allocate their marketing budget more effectively and generate a higher return on investment.

In health and fitness, the Pareto Principle can be applied in many ways to optimize physical health and wellness. One way to apply the principle is by focusing on the 20% of exercises that produce 80% of results. This means identifying the most effective exercises for achieving a specific fitness goal, such as building muscle or increasing cardiovascular endurance, and prioritizing those exercises in a workout routine.

Similarly, the Pareto Principle can be applied to nutrition by focusing on the 20% of foods that provide 80% of nutrients. This involves identifying nutrient-dense foods, such as leafy greens, berries, and nuts, and incorporating them into a balanced and healthy diet. By focusing on the most nutritious foods, individuals can improve their overall health and well-being.

Another way to apply the Pareto Principle in health and fitness is by focusing on the 20% of lifestyle habits that provide 80% of health benefits. These habits may include getting enough sleep, managing stress levels, and engaging in regular physical activity. By prioritizing these habits, individuals can improve their overall health and well-being and reduce their risk of chronic diseases.

In time management, the Pareto Principle can be a useful tool for prioritizing tasks and making the most of one's time. By identifying the 20% of tasks that produce 80% of results, individuals can focus their efforts on the most important and impactful tasks, rather than getting bogged down by less important or time-consuming tasks.

One way to apply the Pareto Principle in time management is to create a to-do list and then rank each task based on its level of importance and potential impact. This allows individuals to identify the tasks that are most likely to yield the greatest results and prioritize them accordingly.

For example, if an individual is working on a project for their job, they may identify the 20% of tasks that are most critical to the project's success, such as developing a clear and concise project plan or delivering a presentation to key stakeholders. By prioritizing these tasks and focusing their time and energy on them, the individual can increase the chances of achieving success in the project.

Similarly, in personal life, the Pareto Principle can be applied to tasks such as household chores or self-improvement goals. By identifying the 20% of tasks that produce 80% of results, individuals can focus their efforts on the most important and impactful tasks, such as decluttering their home or practicing a new skill.

This can help individuals achieve their goals more efficiently and effectively, and can also reduce stress and overwhelm by focusing on the most important tasks first.

The Pareto Principle can be a powerful tool for increasing efficiency and productivity, but it is not the only tool in the productivity toolbox. In this section, we will explore additional tools and techniques that can be used in combination with the Pareto Principle to maximize results with minimal effort.

Time Blocking: Time blocking is a technique that involves scheduling specific blocks of time for certain tasks or activities. By allocating specific times for specific tasks, individuals can better manage their time and increase productivity. Time blocking can be used in conjunction with the Pareto Principle by identifying the 20% of tasks that produce 80% of results and allocating specific blocks of time for these tasks.

Mind Mapping: Mind mapping is a visual tool for organizing thoughts and ideas. By creating a visual map of ideas, individuals can better understand the relationships between different concepts and ideas, leading to increased creativity and productivity. Mind mapping can be used in conjunction with the Pareto Principle by identifying the 20% of ideas that produce 80% of results and organizing them into a visual map.

Kanban Boards: Kanban boards are visual tools for managing workflow and increasing efficiency. By breaking down tasks into smaller, manageable steps and visualizing progress through a kanban board, individuals can better manage their workload and increase productivity. Kanban boards can be used in conjunction with the Pareto Principle by identifying the 20% of tasks that produce 80% of results and visualizing progress through a kanban board.

Pomodoro Technique: The Pomodoro Technique is a time management technique that involves working in 25-minute intervals separated by short breaks. By breaking work down into manageable intervals, individuals can better manage their time and increase productivity. The Pomodoro Technique can be used in conjunction with the Pareto Principle by identifying the 20% of tasks that produce 80% of results and working on them in 25-minute intervals.

It is important to note that while these tools and techniques can be highly effective, they are not without limitations and criticisms. For example, time blocking can be challenging for individuals with unpredictable schedules, while mind mapping may not be suitable for those who are not visually oriented. It is important for individuals to experiment with different tools and techniques to find what works best for their unique needs and circumstances.

While the Pareto Principle can be a powerful tool for maximizing results and improving productivity, it is not without its challenges. Here, we will discuss some common challenges that individuals may face when applying the Pareto Principle and provide strategies and tips for overcoming them.

Difficulty identifying the 20% of causes: One of the primary challenges of the Pareto Principle is identifying the 20% of causes that produce 80% of results. This can be especially difficult when dealing with complex systems or data sets. To overcome this challenge, it can be helpful to break down the data into smaller, more manageable segments and to use visualization tools such as charts or graphs to help identify patterns and trends.

Lack of motivation to implement changes: Another common challenge is a lack of motivation to implement changes based on the Pareto Principle. This may be due to a variety of factors, such as fear of change, a lack of belief in the effectiveness of the principle, or a lack of accountability. To overcome this challenge, it can be helpful to set clear goals and create a plan for implementing changes, as well as to seek support from others, such as a coach or mentor.

Resistance from others: When implementing changes based on the Pareto Principle, there may be resistance from others who are not familiar with the principle or who are resistant to change. To overcome this challenge, it can be helpful to educate others about the principle and its potential benefits, as well as to communicate clearly about the changes being made and why they are important.

Lack of follow-through: Finally, a common challenge is a lack of follow-through on changes made based on the Pareto Principle. This may be due to a lack of accountability or a lack of reinforcement. To overcome this challenge, it can be helpful to track progress and provide regular feedback, as well as to celebrate successes along the way.

Tim Ferriss, the author of "The 4-Hour Workweek," is a well-known advocate of the Pareto Principle. He has written extensively about using the principle to optimize productivity and efficiency in various areas of life. One of his most famous examples of using the principle is in the context of email management.

Ferriss suggests that by identifying the 20% of people who send 80% of your emails, you can focus your attention on those key individuals and reduce the time and effort spent on less important emails. He also recommends setting specific times of the day to check and respond to emails, rather than allowing them to constantly interrupt your workflow.

In addition to email management, Ferriss has applied the Pareto Principle to other areas of life, such as fitness and language learning. For example, he suggests focusing on the 20% of exercises that produce 80% of results, and using tools such as language learning software to focus on the most commonly used words and phrases.

Overall, Tim Ferriss is a great example of someone who has successfully applied the Pareto Principle to multiple areas of life, and his strategies can serve as inspiration for others looking to optimize their productivity and achieve their goals.

In this chapter, we explored the origins and applications of the Pareto Principle, including its use in business, time management, and personal development. We discussed practical tips and strategies for applying the principle, such as identifying the 20% of causes that produce the most impact and prioritizing them for maximum results.

We also discussed additional tools and techniques that can be used in combination with the Pareto Principle, such as visualization tools and mind mapping, to enhance productivity and creativity. We addressed common challenges that individuals may face when using the Pareto Principle, and provided strategies for overcoming these challenges.

Finally, we shared real-life case studies, such as Tim Ferriss and his "Four Hour Work Week," that demonstrate the power of the Pareto Principle in achieving exceptional results with minimal effort.

In conclusion, the Pareto Principle is a valuable tool for anyone looking to optimize their productivity and achieve their goals. We encourage readers to try applying the principle in their own lives and see the potential benefits for themselves.

Chapter 5: A Framework for Personal Development and Success - The Competent Man

The concept of the competent man, also known as the Renaissance man or the polymath, refers to an idealized figure who possesses a diverse range of skills and knowledge across different areas of life. From Leonardo da Vinci to Benjamin Franklin, the idea of the competent man has been celebrated throughout history as a model of excellence and achievement.

In this chapter, we will explore the history and evolution of the competent man archetype, and why it continues to be relevant today. We will examine the potential benefits of striving to become a competent man, such as increased confidence, resilience, and adaptability. We will also discuss practical strategies for developing a wide range of skills and knowledge in different areas of life, and how to maintain a balanced and well-rounded approach to personal development.

By the end of this chapter, readers will have a better understanding of the competent man archetype and how they can apply its principles to their own lives for personal growth and fulfillment.

This section will define the characteristics and skills that define the competent man, including:

Strong communication skills: The competent man is able to effectively communicate with others, both verbally and in writing.

Critical thinking skills: The competent man is able to analyze and evaluate information in a logical and objective manner.

Leadership skills: The competent man is able to inspire and motivate others, and is comfortable taking on leadership roles.

Physical fitness: The competent man takes care of his physical health through exercise and a healthy diet.

Emotional intelligence: The competent man is able to understand and manage his own emotions, as well as those of others.

Examples of historical and contemporary figures who embody the competent man ideal may include Leonardo da Vinci, Theodore Roosevelt, and Elon Musk. These individuals were known for their broad range of skills and knowledge across various fields, as well as their ability to tackle challenges with confidence and adaptability.

To become a competent man, it is essential to have a diverse range of skills across different areas of life. This section will provide practical tips and strategies for developing a diverse skill set and continuously improving oneself.

dentify areas of weakness and set goals: The first step in developing a diverse skill set is to identify areas where you are lacking and set goals for improvement. Start by evaluating your strengths and weaknesses in different areas of life, such as work, relationships, and personal development. Then, set specific goals for acquiring new skills or improving existing ones. It might be worth while using the SMART Goals framework discussed in chapter 1

Once you have identified areas of weakness, it is important to set specific and measurable goals for improvement. These goals should be realistic and achievable, with a clear timeline and action plan for achieving them. For example, if you want to improve your public speaking skills, you might set a goal of attending a public speaking course or practicing your skills in front of a small audience.

There are many resources and tools available for acquiring new skills and knowledge. Online courses, workshops, and books can be useful for learning new skills, while mentorship and networking can help you gain practical experience and insights from others. It is important to find the resources that work best for you and your learning style.

Successful individuals who have developed a diverse skill set often have a growth mindset, which is the belief that their abilities and intelligence can be developed through hard work and dedication. They are not afraid to take risks and embrace failure as a learning opportunity. By setting goals and continually working to improve themselves, they are able to stay adaptable and thrive in a rapidly changing world.

Continuous learning is essential to acquiring new skills and knowledge, and it can help you stay up-to-date with the latest developments in your field. Pursuing continuous learning can take many forms, such as reading books, attending classes or workshops, watching educational videos, or seeking mentorship from experts in your desired fields.
It's also essential to make a habit of setting aside time each day or week for learning and personal development. This may mean dedicating a certain amount of time each day to reading, watching educational videos, or practicing new skills. You can also try setting specific goals for yourself, such as reading one new book each month or attending a workshop every quarter.

To stay motivated, consider joining a group of like-minded individuals who share your interests and goals. This could be a local club or organization, an online community, or a mentorship program. Surrounding yourself with people who are also committed to continuous learning can help keep you accountable and provide support and encouragement along the way.

Ultimately, pursuing continuous learning is a lifelong journey, and it requires a commitment to personal growth and development. But by making learning a priority and seeking out new opportunities for growth, you can develop a diverse range of skills and knowledge that will help you become a competent man.

Networking and collaboration are essential components of becoming a competent man. By connecting with others who share your interests and passions, you can gain new perspectives, learn from their experiences, and develop new skills. Here are some practical tips and strategies for networking and collaboration:

Attend events and conferences: Look for events and conferences related to your interests and attend them regularly. This will give you the opportunity to meet others who share your passions and to learn from experts in your desired fields.

Join clubs or organizations: Join clubs or organizations related to your interests and become an active member. This will provide opportunities for networking, collaboration, and skill development.

Seek mentorship: Find mentors who have expertise in your desired areas and seek their guidance and advice. This can be a great way to gain new insights and develop new skills.

Collaborate on projects: Look for opportunities to collaborate with others on projects or initiatives that challenge you and push you to develop new skills. This can be a great way to learn from others and to expand your skill set.

Use online networking tools: Use online tools such as LinkedIn or Meetup to connect with others who share your interests and passions. This can be a great way to expand your network and to learn from others in your field.

Remember, networking and collaboration are not just about finding opportunities to develop new skills, but also about building relationships with others who share your passions and interests. By working together, you can achieve more than you could on your own and create a supportive community of like-minded individuals.

The competent man archetype can provide a framework for individuals to navigate challenges and uncertainty in various areas of life. By cultivating a diverse skill set and a mindset of continuous learning, individuals can develop the confidence and resilience needed to face difficult situations.

One strategy for navigating challenges is to stay calm under pressure. This can involve taking a step back to assess the situation, breaking down the problem into manageable pieces, and focusing on the most important tasks at hand. It can also involve practicing mindfulness or other relaxation techniques to reduce stress and anxiety.

Another strategy is to adapt to changing circumstances. The competent man is able to pivot and adjust plans as needed, rather than becoming stuck in a rigid mindset. This may involve being open to new ideas and perspectives, as well as being willing to take calculated risks when necessary.

Effective problem-solving is also a key skill for the competent man. This can involve using a systematic approach, such as breaking down the problem into smaller components, gathering information, and considering multiple solutions. It may also involve seeking out the input and advice of others, especially those with expertise in the relevant areas.

Examples of individuals who have used their competence to overcome challenges and achieve their goals can provide inspiration and guidance for others. For example, entrepreneur Elon Musk has demonstrated his competence by successfully launching multiple innovative companies and developing groundbreaking technology. He has faced challenges such as funding shortages, technical setbacks, and public skepticism, but has persevered through his competence and willingness to take risks.

s the CEO of multiple companies, including Tesla, SpaceX, and The Boring Company, Musk has demonstrated his competence in various areas of life, including engineering, business, and innovation.

One of Musk's greatest challenges was the development of the Tesla Model 3, a more affordable electric car intended to bring sustainable transportation to the masses. Musk faced numerous obstacles, including production delays and quality control issues. However, his competence allowed him to navigate these challenges and ultimately deliver on his promise of a mass-market electric car.

Musk's competence also extends to the field of space exploration, as demonstrated by SpaceX's successful launch and docking of the Crew Dragon spacecraft to the International Space Station. This achievement required a high level of technical and engineering expertise, as well as the ability to navigate complex regulatory and safety requirements.

In addition to his technical competence, Musk has also shown adaptability and problem-solving skills in the face of uncertainty. For example, during the COVID-19 pandemic, Musk shifted production at Tesla's factory to produce ventilators for hospitals in need, demonstrating his ability to pivot and adapt to changing circumstances.

Overall, Elon Musk's competence in multiple areas of life has allowed him to overcome challenges and achieve his goals, making him a prime example of the competent man archetype.

The pursuit of competence is not without its potential pitfalls. One such pitfall is arrogance, where an individual may become overconfident in their abilities, leading to a lack of collaboration or a failure to consider alternative viewpoints. Another potential pitfall is burnout, where an individual may become so focused on developing their skills that they neglect self-care and personal relationships.

To avoid these pitfalls, it is important to balance competence with humility and empathy. This means acknowledging the limits of one's own knowledge and skills and being open to learning from others. It also means maintaining a sense of perspective and recognizing the importance of personal relationships and self-care.

Strategies for balancing competence with humility and empathy include:

Cultivating a growth mindset: A growth mindset is the belief that skills and abilities can be developed through hard work and dedication. This mindset allows individuals to approach challenges as opportunities for growth and learning, rather than as threats to their competence.

Seeking feedback and collaboration: Seeking feedback and collaboration from others can provide valuable insights and perspectives. It can also help to prevent arrogance and encourage open-mindedness.

Practicing self-reflection: Regular self-reflection can help individuals maintain a sense of perspective and avoid burnout. It can also provide opportunities for learning and personal growth.

Maintaining personal relationships: Maintaining strong personal relationships can help individuals maintain a sense of perspective and balance in their lives. It can also provide emotional support during challenging times.

Examples of individuals who have maintained a healthy balance between competence and humility include Bill Gates, who has used his wealth and influence to support global health initiatives, and Warren Buffett, who has pledged to give away the majority of his wealth to philanthropic causes. These individuals have demonstrated a commitment to using their competence for the greater good, while maintaining a sense of humility and empathy.

The competent man archetype has been embodied by numerous historical and contemporary figures who have achieved success in different areas of life.

Benjamin Franklin is a historical figure often cited as an embodiment of the competent man archetype. Born in Boston in 1706, Franklin was a polymath who excelled in multiple areas of life. He is well known for his contributions to science, including his experiments with electricity and his invention of the lightning rod. He was also a prolific writer, journalist, and printer, publishing works such as Poor Richard's Almanack and The Pennsylvania Gazette.

Franklin was deeply involved in politics and was a founding father of the United States. He played a key role in drafting the Declaration of Independence and the U.S. Constitution. In addition to his political and scientific achievements, Franklin was also a successful businessman, owning a printing press and a successful publishing company.

One of the key factors in Franklin's success was his commitment to continuous learning and self-improvement. He was an avid reader and sought out mentorship from experts in various fields. He also believed in the importance of hard work and self-discipline, famously saying, "Early to bed and early to rise, makes a man healthy, wealthy, and wise."

Despite his many accomplishments, Franklin was known for his humility and his commitment to helping others. He believed in the importance of giving back to his community and was involved in numerous philanthropic endeavors.

The competent man archetype represents an ideal of someone who possesses a diverse range of skills and knowledge across various areas of life. Striving to become a competent man can bring benefits such as increased confidence, resilience, and adaptability. To develop a diverse skill set, individuals can identify areas of weakness and set goals for improvement, pursue continuous learning, and network and collaborate with others. Additionally, the competent man can serve as a guide for navigating challenges and uncertainty by staying calm under pressure, adapting to changing circumstances, and problem-solving effectively. However, it is important to balance competence with humility and empathy to avoid the pitfalls of arrogance and burnout. Real-life examples of individuals like Ben Franklin and Elon Musk demonstrate how the competent man archetype can be applied to achieve success in various areas of life. Overall, readers are encouraged to reflect on their own skills and knowledge and identify areas where they can work to become more competent in their lives.

SKILL CHECKLIST

№	ACTIVITIES	☑
1	Write a business plan	
2	Build a wall	
3	Design a website	
4	Cook a meal from scratch	
5	Learn to hunt	
6	Change a lightbulb	
7	Change a diaper	
8	Teach others	
9		
10		
11		
12		
13		
14		
15		
16		
17		
18		
19		
20		

Chapter 6: The Flow State: Unlocking Your Deep Focus and Productivity

The flow state is a psychological state of deep focus and productivity that is achieved when engaging in activities that challenge and stimulate us. When in this state, individuals experience heightened concentration, creativity, and a sense of timelessness. The benefits of entering the flow state include increased performance, improved well-being, and a sense of fulfillment.

The flow state is relevant in various areas of life, such as work, sports, and creative pursuits. It can help individuals overcome obstacles, achieve goals, and find enjoyment in their endeavors.

The purpose of this chapter is to provide a comprehensive understanding of the flow state, including its definition, benefits, and practical techniques for entering and sustaining it.

Readers can expect to learn about the science behind the flow state, the benefits of entering it, and strategies for cultivating it in their own lives.

The flow state is a mental state where a person is fully immersed in an activity, experiencing deep focus and productivity. This state can be achieved through a framework that involves several key elements. In this chapter, we will identify and explain these elements, including clear goals, immediate feedback, and optimal challenge.

Clear goals are essential in achieving the flow state. Without clear goals, a person may lose focus and become distracted. By setting clear and specific goals, individuals can maintain their focus and stay on track. When setting goals, it is important to make them achievable yet challenging. This leads us to the second key element, optimal challenge.

Optimal challenge refers to the balance between skill level and the difficulty of the task. When a task is too easy, a person will become bored and disengaged. On the other hand, if a task is too difficult, a person may become overwhelmed and frustrated. The optimal challenge is finding the sweet spot between the two, where a person feels challenged but not overwhelmed.

Immediate feedback is another crucial element in achieving the flow state. Feedback allows individuals to make adjustments in real-time, improving their performance and enhancing their experience. This feedback can be internal or external. Internal feedback involves monitoring your own progress, while external feedback involves receiving feedback from others.

One potential risk is becoming too reliant on the flow state as the sole means of achieving success. This can lead to neglecting other important aspects of productivity such as time management, goal-setting, and prioritization. In order to mitigate this risk, it is important to use the flow state as a complementary tool rather than a replacement for other productivity strategies.

Another potential limitation is the difficulty in achieving and maintaining the flow state consistently. While the flow state can greatly enhance productivity, it is not always possible or practical to enter this state on demand. It is important to recognize that the flow state is not a panacea for all productivity issues and to be flexible in adapting to changing circumstances.

Additionally, the flow state framework may not be suitable for all types of tasks or individuals. Some individuals may find it difficult to enter the flow state for certain types of tasks or in certain environments. It is important to recognize individual differences and to experiment with different strategies to find what works best for each person and situation.

In order to mitigate these risks, it is important to maintain a balance between using the flow state framework and other productivity strategies, to be flexible in adapting to changing circumstances, and to recognize individual differences and adapt accordingly. By doing so, individuals can harness the power of the flow state while minimizing potential drawbacks and limitations.

Chapter 7: The Growth Mindset: Unlocking Your Potential Through Effort and Resilience

The Growth Mindset is a concept developed by psychologist Carol Dweck that refers to the belief that intelligence and abilities can be developed through effort and learning. Individuals with a growth mindset are more likely to embrace challenges, view failures as opportunities for growth, and focus on effort rather than innate abilities.

The concept of the growth mindset originated from Dweck's research on achievement and success, and has since gained widespread attention in fields such as education, sports, and business. By developing a growth mindset, individuals can unlock their full potential and achieve greater success in various areas of life.

In this chapter, we will explore the concept of the growth mindset in detail, discussing its origins, benefits, and practical applications. We will also provide strategies and tips for developing a growth mindset, as well as real-life examples of individuals who have successfully cultivated this mindset to achieve their goals.

The growth mindset is a way of thinking that embraces challenges, views failures as opportunities for growth, and focuses on effort rather than innate abilities. Understanding the key characteristics of a growth mindset, the contrast with a fixed mindset, and the neuroscience behind it can help individuals develop a growth mindset and reap the associated benefits.

Characteristics of a Growth Mindset:

People with a growth mindset tend to possess the following characteristics:

Embrace Challenges: Individuals with a growth mindset view challenges as opportunities to learn and grow rather than as threats to their abilities or ego.

Perseverance: They are persistent in the face of setbacks and obstacles and do not give up easily.

Love of Learning: They enjoy learning and are open to new experiences and knowledge.

Resilience: They are able to bounce back from failures and setbacks, and use these experiences as opportunities for growth.

Focus on Effort: They believe that success is a result of hard work and effort, rather than just natural talent or abilities.

The concept of a fixed mindset is the polar opposite of a growth mindset. While a growth mindset sees challenges and failures as opportunities for learning and growth, a fixed mindset sees them as indications of one's limitations and shortcomings.

Individuals with a fixed mindset believe that their abilities and intelligence are predetermined and cannot be improved. They often avoid challenges or opportunities that may expose their perceived weaknesses, and are more likely to give up when faced with obstacles.

In contrast, individuals with a growth mindset view challenges and failures as opportunities to learn and improve. They believe that their abilities can be developed through dedication, hard work, and perseverance. They embrace challenges and are more resilient in the face of obstacles.

It's important to note that individuals may not have a fixed or growth mindset in all aspects of their lives. For example, someone may have a growth mindset in their career but a fixed mindset in their personal relationships. Recognizing these patterns can help individuals identify areas where they may need to cultivate a growth mindset.

Research in neuroscience has shown that having a growth mindset can physically change the brain. People with a growth mindset have been found to have increased neural connections and activity in the brain's learning and decision-making regions. This suggests that individuals with a growth mindset are better equipped to learn and adapt to new situations.

In contrast, individuals with a fixed mindset have been found to have decreased neural activity in the learning and decision-making regions of the brain. This suggests that they may be less willing to take risks and less able to learn from their mistakes.

Additionally, studies have shown that individuals with a growth mindset have increased levels of the neurotransmitter dopamine, which is associated with motivation and reward. This suggests that individuals with a growth mindset may be more motivated to learn and take on challenges.

To develop a growth mindset, individuals can follow several key practices.

Embrace Challenges : Embracing challenges can be a daunting task, especially when it involves stepping out of one's comfort zone. However, it is an essential step in developing a growth mindset. When individuals push themselves out of their comfort zone and take on new challenges, they are more likely to experience personal growth and development.

There are several ways that individuals can embrace challenges in their daily lives. For example, they can try learning a new skill, taking on a new project at work, or even attempting a new recipe in the kitchen. It's important to remember that challenges don't have to be monumental to be effective. Even small challenges can be an opportunity for growth and development.

When embracing challenges, it's important to approach them with a positive attitude and a willingness to learn. This means being open to making mistakes and being willing to try again when things don't go as planned. Embracing challenges with a growth mindset can lead to increased self-confidence, a sense of accomplishment, and the ability to take on even bigger challenges in the future.

For example, someone who wants to develop a growth mindset might take up a new hobby that challenges them, such as learning a new language or taking up a sport they've never tried before. They may also seek out new experiences, such as traveling to a new country or volunteering for a cause they're passionate about. By embracing these challenges, they can develop new skills, learn more about themselves, and build resilience in the face of adversity.

Focus On Effort Over Ability : focusing on effort over abilities is a crucial aspect of developing a growth mindset. Individuals with a growth mindset believe that their abilities and talents can be developed through hard work, practice, and dedication, rather than being fixed and unchangeable. This mindset encourages individuals to approach challenges with a sense of curiosity and a willingness to learn, rather than a fear of failure or a need to prove their abilities.

To develop a focus on effort, individuals can start by setting specific, achievable goals for themselves that require sustained effort and practice. They can also seek out feedback from others to help identify areas where they can improve and develop new skills. Rather than comparing themselves to others, individuals with a growth mindset focus on their own progress and development, and celebrate their successes along the way.

For example, someone who wants to develop a growth mindset in their professional life might set a goal to learn a new programming language or develop a new skill related to their job. They might break down this goal into smaller, achievable steps and commit to practicing regularly. They might also seek out feedback from their colleagues or a mentor to help identify areas where they can improve and develop new skills. By focusing on effort and dedication, individuals can develop a growth mindset and achieve their goals with resilience and determination.

Develop Resilience : Developing resilience is an essential component of cultivating a growth mindset. To cultivate resilience, individuals can take several steps such as reframing challenges, practicing gratitude, and building a support network.

Reframing challenges involves changing one's perspective to see challenges as opportunities for growth and learning rather than as obstacles to overcome. This shift in mindset can help individuals build confidence and resilience, as they begin to see setbacks as temporary and surmountable.

Practicing gratitude is another way to cultivate resilience. By focusing on what they are grateful for, individuals can shift their attention away from negative emotions and experiences, and instead develop a more positive outlook. This can help individuals feel more motivated and energized, even in the face of difficult challenges.

Building a support network is also crucial for developing resilience. Having a group of supportive friends, family members, or colleagues can provide individuals with the encouragement and motivation they need to keep going during difficult times. This network can offer guidance, feedback, and emotional support, which can help individuals maintain a positive outlook and overcome obstacles.

By cultivating resilience, individuals can develop a sense of self-efficacy and confidence that can help them overcome challenges and achieve their goals. This mindset can be especially important in today's rapidly changing world, where individuals are often faced with uncertainty and unpredictability.

A growth mindset can be applied in various contexts to achieve success and personal growth. Some of the areas where a growth mindset can be particularly useful include:

Education : To apply a growth mindset in education, students can start by seeking out challenging opportunities to learn and grow, such as taking on difficult assignments or pursuing extracurricular activities that stretch their abilities. When faced with setbacks or mistakes, they can view them as opportunities to learn and improve, rather than as reflections of their inherent abilities or worth as a student.

Teachers and educators can also play a role in fostering a growth mindset in their students by providing opportunities for challenge and growth, and by emphasizing effort and hard work over innate abilities. This can involve creating a classroom environment that encourages risk-taking and exploration, and providing feedback that focuses on progress and improvement rather than grades or performance.

Additionally, schools and educational institutions can incorporate the principles of a growth mindset into their curriculum and teaching strategies. This can involve teaching students about the brain's ability to grow and change through experience and practice, and providing opportunities for students to reflect on their own learning and growth. By embracing a growth mindset in education, students can develop the skills and resilience they need to succeed not just in school, but in their future careers and personal lives as well.

Work : To apply a growth mindset in business and career development, individuals can focus on continuously learning and developing new skills, seeking out feedback, and embracing challenges. By seeking out new experiences and opportunities for growth, individuals can expand their knowledge and skills, and become more adaptable and resilient in the face of change.

For example, a person who wants to develop a growth mindset in their career might take on new responsibilities or projects outside of their comfort zone. They may also seek out mentorship or coaching from more experienced colleagues or industry experts to help them develop new skills and insights.

Additionally, individuals can view failures and setbacks as opportunities for learning and growth, rather than as signs of inadequacy or failure. By embracing mistakes and using them as opportunities to reflect and improve, individuals can build a stronger sense of self-efficacy and resilience, which can ultimately lead to greater success and fulfillment in their careers.

Athletics & Sports : Athletes who embrace a growth mindset also tend to focus on the process of training and improving, rather than solely on winning or achieving a certain outcome. This approach can help athletes stay motivated and engaged, even when they encounter setbacks or face tough competition. Additionally, athletes with a growth mindset are often more open to feedback and willing to make changes to their training regimen or technique in order to improve.

For example, a track and field athlete with a growth mindset may not initially have the natural speed of their competitors, but they can still focus on improving their technique and building their endurance through consistent training. By embracing challenges and viewing setbacks as opportunities for growth, they can make steady progress and ultimately become a stronger, more skilled athlete.

A growth mindset can also be helpful in team sports, as it encourages individuals to focus on their own growth and development, while also supporting and collaborating with their teammates. This can create a positive team dynamic, where individuals are motivated to work hard and support each other in pursuit of a common goal.

Tools and Techniques for Developing a Growth Mindset

Developing a growth mindset requires consistent effort and intentional practice. Fortunately, there are several tools and techniques that individuals can use to develop and strengthen their growth mindset:

Self-Reflection and Self-Talk: Self-reflection and self-talk can be powerful tools for developing a growth mindset. By reflecting on past experiences and analyzing the ways in which they can learn and grow from them, individuals can cultivate a sense of self-awareness and resilience. Positive self-talk, such as affirmations and encouragement, can also help individuals build self-confidence and focus on their efforts and progress rather than their perceived limitations.

Goal-Setting and Tracking Progress: Goal-setting and tracking progress can also be effective tools for developing a growth mindset. By setting specific, measurable goals and tracking their progress over time, individuals can maintain a sense of motivation and focus, and feel a sense of accomplishment as they achieve their goals. Additionally, breaking larger goals down into smaller, more manageable steps can help individuals feel less overwhelmed and more confident in their ability to achieve their objectives.

Seeking Feedback and Mentorship: Seeking feedback and mentorship from others can also be beneficial for developing a growth mindset. By receiving constructive criticism and guidance from others, individuals can gain new perspectives and insights, and identify areas where they can improve their skills and abilities. Mentors can also serve as role models and sources of inspiration, offering support and encouragement as individuals pursue their goals and aspirations.

Gratitude and Mindfulness Practices: Gratitude and mindfulness practices can also be effective tools for developing a growth mindset. By focusing on the present moment and practicing gratitude for the opportunities and experiences they have, individuals can cultivate a sense of positivity and resilience. Mindfulness practices, such as meditation or deep breathing exercises, can also help individuals manage stress and anxiety, and stay focused and grounded as they work to develop their growth mindset.

After understanding the importance and benefits of having a growth mindset, there are several key takeaways that individuals can consider:

Embrace challenges as opportunities for growth and learning.
Focus on effort and perseverance rather than innate abilities or talent.
View setbacks and failures as opportunities for learning and growth.

Cultivate resilience and a positive attitude towards challenges.

To develop a growth mindset, individuals can apply several tools and techniques, such as self-reflection and self-talk, goal-setting and tracking progress, seeking feedback and mentorship, and practicing gratitude and mindfulness.

It is important to recognize that developing a growth mindset is a continuous process that requires ongoing effort and dedication. By embracing a growth mindset, individuals can experience greater success and fulfillment in various areas of their lives.

Chapter 8: Assessing Your Strategic Position: The SWOT Analysis Framework

In today's fast-paced and competitive world, it's important for individuals and businesses to make informed decisions that can help them achieve their goals. One effective tool for decision-making and planning is the SWOT analysis.

A SWOT analysis is a framework for analyzing the strengths, weaknesses, opportunities, and threats in a given situation or context. By identifying and analyzing these four factors, individuals and organizations can gain a better understanding of their current situation and make strategic decisions that can help them achieve their objectives.

The SWOT analysis framework has been around for several decades and has evolved over time. It was first introduced in the 1960s by management consultant Albert Humphrey, who developed the tool as part of a research project for the Stanford Research Institute. Since then, the SWOT analysis has become a popular and widely used tool in various fields, including business, education, and personal development.

The importance of using a SWOT analysis in decision-making and planning cannot be overstated. It can help individuals and organizations to identify areas where they excel and where they need improvement, as well as opportunities for growth and potential threats to their success.

One of the strengths of the SWOT analysis is its simplicity and flexibility. It can be used in various contexts and can be adapted to suit different needs and objectives.

In the following chapters, we will dive deeper into the SWOT analysis framework and explore each of the four factors in detail. We will also provide practical tips and strategies for conducting a SWOT analysis and applying the insights gained from the analysis to decision-making and planning processes.

One of the key benefits of using SWOT analysis in decision-making and planning is that it allows you to take a comprehensive and objective look at your situation. It helps you identify the internal factors that are within your control, such as your strengths and weaknesses, as well as the external factors that may be beyond your control, such as market trends or regulatory changes.

Strengths:
When conducting a SWOT analysis, it is important to start with strengths. Strengths refer to the internal attributes of your organization or personal situation that give you a competitive advantage or contribute to your success. These may include:

Expertise and knowledge: Your organization or personal situation may have unique expertise or knowledge that sets you apart from your competitors. This may be a specialized skill set, a unique perspective, or a deep understanding of a particular industry or market.

Strong brand reputation: A strong brand reputation can be a significant strength for organizations and individuals alike. A positive brand reputation can increase customer loyalty, attract new customers, and help you stand out in a crowded market.

Financial resources: Having strong financial resources can provide a significant advantage when pursuing business or personal goals. This may include access to funding, cash reserves, or investments that can be used to fuel growth and innovation.

Strong partnerships and collaborations: Strong partnerships and collaborations can help you leverage the expertise and resources of others to achieve your goals. By working together, you can achieve greater success than you would on your own.

How to identify and evaluate strengths using SWOT analysis:
To identify and evaluate your strengths using SWOT analysis, start by asking yourself the following questions:

What are the internal attributes of my organization or personal situation that give me a competitive advantage or contribute to my success?
What do I do better than my competitors or peers?

What resources do I have that can help me achieve my goals?

What unique expertise or knowledge do I possess?

Once you have identified your strengths, evaluate them by considering their impact on your goals and objectives. Ask yourself:

How do my strengths contribute to my ability to achieve my goals?

How can I leverage my strengths to overcome challenges and obstacles?

Are there any potential weaknesses or threats that could undermine my strengths?

Strategies for leveraging strengths to achieve goals and overcome challenges:

Once you have identified and evaluated your strengths, the next step is to leverage them to achieve your goals and overcome challenges. Here are a few strategies to consider:

Focus on your core strengths: Identify the strengths that are most relevant to your goals and objectives, and focus on developing and leveraging them.

Seek out opportunities that align with your strengths: Look for opportunities that allow you to use your strengths to your advantage. This may include pursuing projects or partnerships that align with your expertise, or targeting markets or customer segments that value your unique attributes.

Mitigate weaknesses and threats: While it's important to focus on your strengths, it's also important to mitigate weaknesses and

In the context of SWOT analysis, weaknesses are identified through a critical evaluation of internal factors that could hinder progress towards achieving goals or objectives.

Some examples of weaknesses in a business context include outdated technology, poor financial management, lack of marketing expertise, and inadequate employee training. On a personal level, weaknesses could include poor time management, procrastination, lack of assertiveness, or limited communication skills.

To identify weaknesses, individuals or businesses should reflect on past experiences and current practices to determine areas that need improvement. This can be done through self-reflection, feedback from others, and analysis of performance metrics or financial reports.

Once weaknesses have been identified, strategies can be developed to address them. For businesses, this may involve investing in new technology, implementing new management processes, or providing additional training to employees. For individuals, strategies may involve seeking mentorship or coaching, taking courses to develop new skills, or developing a personal development plan.

By identifying and addressing weaknesses through SWOT analysis, individuals and businesses can become more self-aware and better equipped to achieve their goals and objectives. It can also help in mitigating potential risks and challenges that could arise due to the identified weaknesses.

Opportunities refer to external factors or circumstances that could be advantageous to an individual or an organization in achieving their goals. These could be new markets, emerging technologies, partnerships, or other favorable conditions that can be leveraged to create value or gain a competitive advantage.

To identify and evaluate opportunities using SWOT analysis, individuals or organizations should consider the following:

Market trends: Identify emerging trends in the market and evaluate whether they present opportunities for growth or expansion.

Competitor analysis: Analyze the strengths and weaknesses of competitors to identify potential gaps in the market that can be exploited.

New technologies: Stay abreast of new technologies and evaluate whether they can be leveraged to improve products or services, reduce costs, or enhance processes.

Regulatory changes: Monitor changes in laws and regulations that could create new opportunities or impact existing operations.

Partnerships and collaborations: Identify potential partners or collaborators who can help expand the reach or capabilities of the organization.

Examples of opportunities in a business context could include expanding into new markets, launching new products or services, forming strategic partnerships, or adopting new technologies. In a personal context, opportunities could include pursuing new hobbies or interests, exploring new career paths, or developing new skills.

hreats refer to external factors or challenges that can potentially harm the business or individual's performance. It is essential to identify and analyze these threats to create contingency plans and mitigate potential risks.

In a business context, threats can be anything from changing market trends to increased competition, economic downturns, and government regulations. For instance, a startup company may face threats from established players in the market, while a well-established company may face threats from disruptive technologies that can change the market dynamics.

In a personal context, threats can include anything that may affect the individual's ability to achieve their goals. For example, an individual looking to pursue a career change may face threats such as a lack of relevant experience or stiff competition in the job market.

To identify and evaluate threats, individuals can consider external factors that may pose a challenge to their goals. This can include analyzing market trends, researching competitors, and identifying potential changes in economic, political, or environmental factors.

Once the threats have been identified, individuals can develop contingency plans and strategies to mitigate the potential risks. This can involve investing in new technologies, diversifying the business, or developing new skills to remain competitive in the market. In a personal context, it may involve pursuing additional education or training, seeking mentorship or guidance, or exploring alternative career options.

By identifying and evaluating threats using SWOT analysis, individuals can proactively anticipate potential challenges and take action to mitigate the risks. This can ultimately help them achieve their goals and ensure long-term success.

To conduct a successful SWOT analysis, there are certain best practices that should be followed. These include:

Identify the purpose and scope of the analysis: Before beginning a SWOT analysis, it is important to clearly define the purpose and scope of the analysis. This will help ensure that the analysis is focused and targeted towards the specific goals and objectives of the organization or individual.

Gather relevant information: To conduct an effective SWOT analysis, it is important to gather relevant information about the internal and external factors that may impact the organization or individual. This may include data on market trends, customer behavior, competitor activity, and financial performance, among other factors.

Use a SWOT analysis template: Using a SWOT analysis template can help organize the information gathered and ensure that all relevant factors are considered. The template should include four sections for strengths, weaknesses, opportunities, and threats, as well as space for notes and analysis.

Analyze and prioritize the factors: Once all relevant factors have been identified, it is important to analyze and prioritize them. This may involve assessing the impact and likelihood of each factor, as well as considering the organization or individual's strengths and weaknesses in relation to each factor.

Develop an action plan: Finally, based on the results of the SWOT analysis, it is important to develop an action plan that outlines specific steps and strategies for leveraging strengths, addressing weaknesses, capitalizing on opportunities, and mitigating threats.

Tools and Resources for Effective SWOT Analysis

There are a variety of tools and resources available to help individuals and organizations conduct effective SWOT analyses. These may include:

SWOT analysis templates: There are a number of free SWOT analysis templates available online that can be used to guide the analysis process and ensure that all relevant factors are considered.

Market research reports: Market research reports can provide valuable insights into market trends, customer behavior, and competitor activity that can inform a SWOT analysis.

Data analysis software: Data analysis software, such as Excel or Tableau, can be used to organize and analyze large amounts of data, making it easier to identify patterns and trends.

SWOT analysis training: Many business schools and professional development programs offer training in SWOT analysis, providing individuals with the knowledge and skills necessary to conduct effective analyses.

Limitations and Criticisms of SWOT Analysis

While SWOT analysis can be a useful tool for decision-making and planning, it is important to recognize its limitations and potential criticisms. These may include:

Lack of objectivity: SWOT analysis is subjective and can be influenced by personal biases and opinions, which may impact the accuracy and reliability of the analysis.

Overemphasis on internal factors: SWOT analysis tends to focus on internal factors, such as strengths and weaknesses, at the expense of external factors, such as market trends and competitor activity.

Incomplete analysis: SWOT analysis is often conducted in isolation, without considering other factors or strategies that may impact the organization or individual.

Lack of action-oriented outcomes: While SWOT analysis can provide valuable insights into an organization or individual's situation, it does not necessarily lead to action-oriented outcomes or specific recommendations for improvement.

There are also alternative frameworks for analyzing situations and making decisions that may be more suitable in certain contexts. For example, Porter's Five Forces analysis can be used to evaluate the competitive landscape of an industry, while PEST analysis can be used to evaluate external factors such as political, economic, social, and technological trends.

Despite its limitations, there are strategies for addressing these criticisms and improving the effectiveness of SWOT analysis. One strategy is to involve multiple stakeholders in the analysis process to ensure a diversity of perspectives. Another strategy is to conduct a thorough analysis of each factor and provide evidence to support each conclusion. Finally, it is important to regularly review and update the SWOT analysis to ensure it remains relevant and useful.

The SWOT analysis is a versatile and valuable tool that can help individuals and organizations evaluate their strengths, weaknesses, opportunities, and threats. By conducting a SWOT analysis, individuals and businesses can make informed decisions, develop effective strategies, and achieve their goals. However, as with any tool, SWOT analysis has its limitations and critics. It is important to use SWOT analysis in conjunction with other frameworks and strategies to ensure that the analysis is comprehensive and effective.

SWOT ANALYSIS

STRENGTHS	WEAKNESS

OPPORTUNITIES	THREATS

Chapter 9: The Four Tendencies: Understanding Personality Types for Better Communication and Decision-Making

The Four Tendencies framework is a personality framework that was developed by author and speaker Gretchen Rubin. It identifies four different personality types and how they respond to expectations, both internal and external. The four tendencies are: Upholder, Obliger, Questioner, and Rebel. An Upholder is someone who responds readily to both inner and outer expectations, while an Obliger responds readily to outer expectations but struggles with meeting inner expectations. A Questioner questions all expectations, and will only meet them if they believe they are justified. A Rebel resists all expectations, and will only do something if they feel like doing it. Understanding these personality types can be incredibly useful in personal and professional contexts, as it can help individuals better understand themselves and those around them. By understanding their own tendency, individuals can identify strategies that work best for them in terms of motivation and accountability, and can also learn how to better communicate and work with others who have different tendencies.

The Four Tendencies framework was developed by Gretchen Rubin, a writer and speaker who specializes in happiness and human nature. Rubin's inspiration for the framework came from her observation that people respond to expectations in different ways. Through her research, Rubin identified four distinct personality types based on how individuals respond to both internal and external expectations. She named these personality types Upholders, Questioners, Obligers, and Rebels. Upholders are those who readily meet both internal and external expectations, while Questioners question all expectations and only meet them if they make sense to them. Obligers are those who readily meet external expectations but struggle with meeting internal expectations, and Rebels resist all expectations and often do the opposite of what is expected.

The Four Tendencies framework has evolved since its initial introduction, with Rubin continuing to refine and expand upon it in her subsequent books and articles. She has also developed online quizzes and other tools to help individuals identify their tendency and learn more about how to use this knowledge to improve their lives. The framework has been applied in various contexts, from personal growth and relationships to workplace productivity and management. By understanding the Four Tendencies framework and how it applies to different individuals, we can better understand ourselves and others, and tailor our approaches to expectations and communication accordingly.

Understanding personality types can be valuable in both personal and professional contexts. It can help individuals communicate more effectively with others, manage conflicts, and set goals that are aligned with their strengths and motivations

The Four Tendencies framework identifies four different personality types:

Upholders: Upholders are individuals who respond well to both internal and external expectations. They are self-motivated and highly reliable, and tend to be good at meeting deadlines and following through on commitments.

Questioners: Questioners are individuals who are highly motivated by internal expectations, but are less responsive to external expectations. They tend to be highly analytical and independent thinkers, and may question rules and conventions that they see as arbitrary or illogical.

Obligers: Obligers are individuals who are highly motivated by external expectations, but may struggle to meet internal expectations. They tend to be highly responsive to the needs and expectations of others, and may need external accountability and support to meet their own goals and commitments.

Rebels: Rebels are individuals who resist both internal and external expectations. They tend to be highly independent and value their own freedom and autonomy, and may struggle with authority and rules that they see as limiting.

Understanding these personality types can help individuals better understand their own motivations and behaviors, as well as those of others. In the following chapters, we will explore each of these tendencies in more detail, and discuss strategies for working effectively with each type.

Understanding The Four Tendencies can be useful in personal and professional contexts. For example, employers can use the framework to tailor their management and communication styles to the individual needs of their employees. In personal relationships, understanding the tendencies of others can help improve communication and reduce conflict. Individuals can also use the framework to better understand their own tendencies and develop strategies for setting and achieving goals.

There are several strategies for identifying one's own tendency within the Four Tendencies framework. Firstly, it involves understanding the key characteristics and behavior patterns associated with each of the four tendencies. For example, individuals with an Upholder tendency are typically self-motivated and driven to meet both internal and external expectations, while those with an Obliger tendency may struggle with meeting internal expectations but thrive under external accountability. Understanding these general tendencies can provide a starting point for self-reflection and identifying one's own patterns of behavior.

Another aspect of identifying one's own tendency involves analyzing how one responds to both internal and external expectations. This may involve reflecting on past experiences and situations where one may have struggled or excelled in meeting expectations. It may also involve evaluating one's own decision-making process and considering the factors that influence one's choices.

Lastly, taking a quiz or assessment can be a helpful tool for determining one's own tendency. Several online quizzes and assessments are available that use a series of questions and scenarios to determine an individual's tendency. While these quizzes should not be relied on solely for identifying one's tendency, they can provide a helpful starting point for further self-reflection and exploration.

Strategies for identifying someone else's tendency involve observing their behavior and communication style. By paying attention to how they respond to expectations and the language they use to describe their preferences and decision-making, it is possible to make an educated guess about their tendency. Additionally, asking questions and engaging in open communication can provide valuable insights into a person's personality type. It is important to approach the identification process with an open mind and avoid making assumptions or judgments based on limited information.

Effective communication with individuals of different tendencies requires a deep understanding of their needs, motivations, and preferred communication styles. For instance, those with an Upholder tendency respond well to clear expectations and timelines, and prefer working in structured environments where they can follow rules and guidelines. In contrast, those with a Rebel tendency prefer autonomy and creativity in their work, and may resist being told what to do.

Those with an Obliger tendency thrive on accountability and external expectations, and may struggle with self-motivation. As such, they may benefit from clear deadlines, regular check-ins, and external accountability. Finally, individuals with a Questioner tendency require a lot of information and rationale before they can commit to a decision or task. They may also be resistant to following rules and guidelines that they perceive as arbitrary or pointless.

Adapting communication styles to meet the needs of individuals with different tendencies can help build strong relationships and foster productive collaboration. It may also be helpful to provide appropriate levels of support and guidance, depending on the individual's tendency. For example, an Obliger may benefit from a clear accountability system, while a Rebel may appreciate more creative and flexible work arrangements.

By understanding the different tendencies and adapting communication and support strategies accordingly, individuals can work more effectively with others and create more harmonious personal and professional relationships.

Applying The Four Tendencies in personal and professional contexts involves using the framework as a tool for personal growth and development. For example, understanding one's own tendency can help individuals identify their strengths and weaknesses, and develop strategies for building better habits and achieving their goals. In a business setting, understanding the tendencies of colleagues and team members can help to improve communication, collaboration, and overall performance.

In conclusion, The Four Tendencies framework provides a useful tool for understanding how different individuals respond to internal and external expectations. By identifying one's own tendency and understanding the tendencies of those around us, we can improve communication and work more effectively with others. Real-life examples have demonstrated how the framework can be applied in personal and professional contexts to improve relationships and achieve better outcomes. However, it is important to acknowledge the limitations and criticisms of the framework, including the potential for oversimplification and the possibility of individuals exhibiting traits from multiple tendencies. Overall, The Four Tendencies framework provides a valuable lens for understanding human behavior and can be a useful tool for personal and professional growth.

Chapter 10: Mastering the Art of Effective Decision-Making - The OODA Loop

The OODA Loop is a decision-making and action framework developed by military strategist and United States Air Force Colonel John Boyd. The framework involves four stages: Observe, Orient, Decide, and Act. The purpose of the OODA Loop is to provide a structured process for making decisions and taking action in high-stress or fast-paced situations, such as military operations or emergency response situations.

The framework has since been adapted for use in various other contexts, including business, sports, and personal decision-making. Understanding and utilizing the OODA Loop can help individuals and organizations make more informed decisions, act more quickly and decisively, and adapt to changing circumstances.

Observe Stage:

The first stage of the OODA Loop is the Observe stage, which involves gathering information about the situation or problem at hand. This includes gathering data, analyzing patterns and trends, and identifying potential challenges or risks. The goal of the Observe stage is to gain a thorough understanding of the situation before moving on to the next stage.

The Observe stage can be especially important in fast-paced or high-pressure situations where decisions need to be made quickly. By taking the time to observe and gather information, individuals and organizations can make more informed decisions that are based on a comprehensive understanding of the situation.

However, it is important to note that the Observe stage can also be a source of delay or inaction if individuals or organizations become too focused on gathering information and fail to move on to the next stages of the framework. It is important to strike a balance between thorough observation and timely action.

Orient Stage:

The second stage of the OODA Loop is the Orient stage, which involves analyzing and interpreting the information gathered in the

Observe stage. This includes identifying patterns and relationships between different data points, and assessing the potential impact of different factors on the situation at hand.

The goal of the Orient stage is to develop a clear understanding of the situation and to identify potential courses of action. This requires individuals and organizations to use critical thinking skills and to draw on their knowledge and experience to make sense of the information gathered in the Observe stage.

The Orient stage is especially important in complex or rapidly changing situations where there may be multiple factors to consider. By taking the time to analyze and interpret the information gathered in the Observe stage, individuals and organizations can make more informed decisions that are based on a deep understanding of the situation.

However, like the Observe stage, the Orient stage can also be a source of delay or inaction if individuals or organizations become too focused on analysis and fail to move on to the next stages of the framework. It is important to strike a balance between analysis and action.

Decide Stage:

The third stage of the OODA Loop is the Decide stage, which involves choosing a course of action based on the information gathered in the Observe and Orient stages. This requires individuals and organizations to weigh the potential risks and benefits of different options and to make a decision that is likely to lead to the best possible outcome.

The goal of the Decide stage is to choose a course of action that is both effective and efficient. This requires individuals and organizations to be decisive and to act quickly to implement their chosen course of action.

Act Stage:

The fourth and final stage of the OODA Loop is the Act stage, which involves implementing the chosen course of action. This requires individuals and organizations to take decisive action and to remain flexible and adaptable as circumstances change.

The goal of the Act stage is to achieve the desired outcome and to respond quickly and effectively to any unforeseen challenges or obstacles that may arise. By remaining flexible and adaptable, individuals and organizations can continue to gather information and adjust their actions as necessary to achieve their goals.

The observe stage is the first step in the OODA Loop framework, which involves gathering information and data in order to make informed decisions and take action. The purpose of the observe stage is to gather as much relevant information as possible about the situation at hand, in order to better understand the current reality and potential future outcomes.

Effective observation techniques and tools are crucial in this stage, as they help to ensure that all relevant information is gathered and considered. This may include techniques such as active listening, note-taking, and visual observation, as well as tools such as data analysis software and monitoring systems.

Real-life examples of the observe stage in action can be seen in various contexts, such as law enforcement, military strategy, and scientific research. For instance, a detective investigating a crime scene will carefully observe and document any relevant evidence, while a scientist conducting research will use observation to gather data and test hypotheses.

In order to effectively move on to the next stage of the OODA Loop framework, it is important to have a thorough understanding of the observe stage and its purpose. By gathering and analyzing as much relevant information as possible, individuals can make more informed decisions and take action with greater confidence.

The orient stage is the second stage in the OODA loop framework. It involves analyzing the information gathered in the observe and orient stages to form a decision or plan of action. The purpose of this stage is to understand the situation, identify the possible courses of action, and choose the most appropriate one.

To effectively orient oneself, it is important to analyze the information gathered in the previous stages and understand the context and implications of the situation. This may involve using analytical tools and techniques, such as SWOT analysis or cost-benefit analysis, to assess the options and their potential outcomes.

Real-life examples of the orient stage in action include a military commander analyzing intelligence reports to determine the best course of action in a battle, a business executive evaluating market data to make strategic decisions, and an individual weighing the pros and cons of different job offers before making a decision.

Effective orientation is essential for making informed decisions and taking appropriate actions. By analyzing the available information and understanding the context and implications of the situation, individuals can choose the best course of action and increase their chances of success.

The third stage in the OODA Loop framework is the Decide stage. This stage involves using the information gathered in the Observe and Orient stages to make a decision on how to proceed. The decision-making process can be influenced by a variety of factors, such as the individual's personal values, goals, and objectives.

The purpose of the Decide stage is to use the information and analysis from the previous stages to determine the best course of action. This stage can involve making a single decision or a series of decisions that build upon each other. It is important to note that decisions made in the Decide stage are not necessarily final, as the OODA Loop is a continuous process.

Effective decision-making techniques in the Decide stage include weighing the pros and cons of each option, considering potential risks and consequences, and seeking input from others when appropriate. The decision-making process can also involve setting priorities and creating a plan for implementation.

Real-life examples of the Decide stage in action include a military commander making strategic decisions based on intelligence and analysis, a business executive making decisions about product development based on market research, or an individual making a decision about whether to accept a job offer based on personal goals and values.

The act stage is the final step of the OODA loop and involves putting the decision into action. This stage requires taking the chosen course of action and executing it in a timely and effective manner. The purpose of the act stage is to close the loop and see the results of the decision-making process.

To effectively carry out the act stage, it is important to have clear goals and objectives, establish a plan of action, and implement the plan with the necessary resources and support. Effective communication and coordination among team members or stakeholders is also critical in ensuring the success of the action taken.

There are various techniques and tools that can be used to facilitate effective action and implementation. These include establishing timelines and deadlines, monitoring progress and performance, and adapting the plan as needed based on feedback and results.

Real-life examples of the act stage in action can be seen in various contexts, such as business, military, and emergency response. For instance, a business may use the OODA loop to make a decision about launching a new product and then implement the plan by developing and marketing the product. In the military, the OODA loop is used to guide decision-making in combat situations and executing battle plans. Similarly, emergency responders use the OODA loop to assess and respond to crises and disasters.

After the act stage, it is important to move back to the observe stage and repeat the loop. This allows individuals to continually gather new information, adjust their orientation and decision-making processes, and improve their actions and implementation. By using the OODA loop as a continuous cycle, individuals can remain agile and adaptable in the face of changing circumstances, and make more informed and effective decisions.

Once individuals have a strong understanding of the OODA Loop framework and its four stages, they can begin to apply it in various personal and professional contexts. Some strategies for applying the OODA Loop include:

Emphasizing continuous learning: Effective decision-making and action rely on a deep understanding of the context and environment. By consistently gathering information and analyzing trends, individuals can build a foundation of knowledge that can inform their decision-making.

Prioritizing speed and agility: The OODA Loop emphasizes the importance of acting quickly and decisively. In order to apply the framework effectively, individuals must be willing to make decisions and take action in a timely manner, without getting bogged down in analysis paralysis.

Cultivating a flexible mindset: The OODA Loop emphasizes the importance of remaining flexible and adaptable in the face of change. By staying open to new information and adjusting their plans accordingly, individuals can navigate complex situations more effectively.

Encouraging collaboration and communication: The OODA Loop can be applied more effectively in group settings when individuals work together and share information openly. Encouraging collaboration and effective communication can lead to better decision-making and more successful outcomes.

The OODA Loop framework can lead to better decision-making and outcomes by providing a structured and systematic approach to the decision-making process. One example of how the framework can be applied is in military operations. The framework was originally developed by military strategist John Boyd as a tool for improving combat performance. By using the OODA Loop, military personnel can make quick and effective decisions in rapidly changing and unpredictable situations.

Another example of how the OODA Loop can lead to better outcomes is in business management. The framework can be used to analyze and respond to changes in the market and industry trends. By continuously observing, orienting, deciding, and acting, businesses can stay ahead of the competition and adapt to changing circumstances.

Additionally, the OODA Loop can be applied to personal decision-making, such as in everyday life or in the pursuit of personal goals. By following the four stages of the loop, individuals can make more informed and effective decisions, and take action towards achieving their desired outcomes.

The OODA Loop was originally developed by military strategist and pilot John Boyd. It has been used in military operations to help soldiers make quick and effective decisions in high-stress situations. For example, during the Gulf War, the United States Air Force used the OODA Loop to gain the upper hand against Iraqi forces by making faster decisions and adjusting their strategy more quickly.

Business Strategy: The OODA Loop has been applied in the business world to help leaders make better decisions and respond more quickly to changes in the market. For example, Amazon's CEO Jeff Bezos has credited the OODA Loop as a key component of the company's success. By constantly observing and orienting to changes in the market, Amazon is able to make faster decisions and adapt more quickly to new trends.

Sports Strategy: The OODA Loop has also been used in the world of sports to help athletes make quick and effective decisions on the field. For example, in soccer, players must constantly observe and orient to the movements of their opponents in order to make effective decisions about where to pass the ball or when to make a shot.

Chapter 11: Maximizing Results: Combining Frameworks for Greater Success

n today's fast-paced world, individuals and organizations are constantly seeking ways to improve productivity, efficiency, and decision-making. One way to achieve this is by utilizing various frameworks and techniques that are designed to address specific challenges and goals. However, it is important to note that no single framework can solve all problems or meet all needs. This is where the concept of combining frameworks comes in. By utilizing multiple frameworks together, individuals and organizations can achieve greater results and outcomes.

Applying multiple frameworks involves combining two or more frameworks to address a specific challenge or goal. This can be particularly effective when the frameworks complement each other or address different aspects of the same problem. The importance of applying multiple frameworks lies in the fact that it allows for a more comprehensive approach to problem-solving and decision-making. It also provides the opportunity to leverage the strengths and advantages of different frameworks, while addressing their limitations and weaknesses.

There are numerous frameworks that can be combined to achieve greater results. For example, the Pomodoro Technique can be combined with the Eisenhower Matrix to prioritize tasks and improve time management. The Growth Mindset can be combined with the Pareto Principle to focus on the 20% of efforts that yield 80% of the results. The OODA Loop can be combined with the SWOT Analysis to make informed decisions and take effective action. These are just a few examples of how frameworks can be combined to achieve better results.

This chapter will explore the benefits and strategies of combining frameworks, as well as provide real-life examples of how this approach has been successful in various contexts. It will also address some of the potential challenges and limitations of combining frameworks, and provide guidance on how to navigate these obstacles. By the end of this chapter, readers will have a deeper understanding of the benefits and best practices of applying multiple frameworks to achieve greater outcomes.

When it comes to achieving goals and managing tasks, two commonly used frameworks are SMART Goals and the Eisenhower Matrix. SMART Goals involves setting goals that are Specific, Measurable, Achievable, Relevant, and Time-bound, while the Eisenhower Matrix is a framework for prioritizing tasks based on their importance and urgency.

Combining these frameworks can be a powerful way to improve productivity and achieve better results. By setting SMART goals, individuals can identify specific and relevant tasks that need to be accomplished within a set timeframe. The Eisenhower Matrix can then be used to prioritize these tasks based on their level of urgency and importance. This allows individuals to focus on the most critical tasks first, ensuring that they are accomplished in a timely manner.

For example, if an individual has set a SMART goal of completing a project within a specific timeframe, they can use the Eisenhower Matrix to identify which tasks are most important and urgent in order to meet the deadline. This can help prevent procrastination and ensure that the most critical tasks are accomplished in a timely manner.

In addition to improving productivity, combining these frameworks can also help individuals stay motivated and focused. By setting specific goals and prioritizing tasks, individuals can see tangible progress and feel a sense of accomplishment as they work towards their goals.

Furthermore, combining these frameworks can help individuals develop a sense of purpose and direction in their personal and professional lives. By setting SMART goals and using the Eisenhower Matrix to prioritize tasks, individuals can ensure that they are working towards objectives that are aligned with their values and long-term aspirations.

Another benefit of combining these frameworks is that it can help individuals manage their time more effectively. By setting SMART goals and prioritizing tasks, individuals can avoid wasting time on activities that are not important or relevant to their goals. This can help individuals achieve a better work-life balance and avoid burnout.

When it comes to managing time and increasing productivity, two popular frameworks are the Pomodoro Technique and the Flow State. The Pomodoro Technique is a time-management framework that involves breaking work into 25-minute intervals separated by short breaks, while the Flow State is a framework for achieving a state of deep focus and productivity by engaging in activities that challenge and stimulate you.

Combining these frameworks can be a powerful way to enhance focus and productivity. The Pomodoro Technique can help individuals break down their work into manageable intervals and avoid burnout, while the Flow State can help them achieve a state of deep focus and engagement. By alternating between periods of focused work using the Pomodoro Technique and engaging in activities that stimulate and challenge them, individuals can achieve a state of flow and accomplish more in less time.

For example, an individual can use the Pomodoro Technique to break down a larger task into smaller, manageable intervals and alternate between focused work and taking breaks. During their breaks, they can engage in activities that stimulate and challenge them, such as reading a challenging book or practicing a new skill. This can help them achieve a state of flow and increase their overall productivity and focus.

By combining these frameworks, individuals can achieve a balance between focused work and engaging in activities that stimulate and challenge them. This can help them avoid burnout and achieve a state of flow, leading to increased productivity and a sense of accomplishment.

When it comes to personal growth and development, two frameworks that can be combined are the Growth Mindset and the Four Tendencies. The Growth Mindset is a framework for developing a mindset that embraces challenges, views failures as opportunities for growth, and focuses on effort rather than innate abilities. The Four Tendencies is a personality framework that identifies four different personality types and how they respond to expectations, both internal and external.

By combining these frameworks, individuals can better understand their own tendencies and how they respond to challenges and expectations. This self-awareness can then be used to develop a Growth Mindset, which can help individuals overcome self-limiting beliefs and achieve their goals. For example, an individual who identifies as an Obliger, who responds well to external expectations but struggles with internal expectations, can use the Growth Mindset to develop strategies for overcoming their tendency to put others' needs before their own and prioritize their own goals.

Similarly, understanding the Four Tendencies can also help individuals in developing a Growth Mindset by providing insights into how they respond to challenges and feedback. For example, a Rebel who tends to resist expectations and authority figures may benefit from reframing challenges as opportunities for growth and focusing on the effort needed to overcome them rather than the perceived limitations imposed by others.

By combining the Growth Mindset and the Four Tendencies, individuals can develop a more holistic approach to personal growth and development that takes into account both their innate tendencies and their ability to overcome challenges and achieve their goals. This can lead to greater self-awareness, improved productivity, and a greater sense of fulfillment and purpose.

When combining the Growth Mindset and Four Tendencies frameworks, individuals can develop a better understanding of how different personality types approach challenges and opportunities for growth. By identifying their own tendency and understanding how to effectively communicate and work with others who have different tendencies, individuals can cultivate a growth mindset and focus on effort rather than innate abilities.

For example, individuals with an Upholder tendency may benefit from setting specific goals and tracking their progress, while those with a Questioner tendency may benefit from seeking out new information and challenging assumptions. Meanwhile, individuals with an Obliger tendency may benefit from seeking accountability and support from others, while those with a Rebel tendency may benefit from embracing new and unconventional approaches to problem-solving.

Combining these frameworks can also lead to improved collaboration and teamwork, as individuals with different tendencies can work together to achieve common goals and support each other in their efforts towards personal and professional growth.

Combining the SWOT Analysis and OODA Loop can be particularly useful in decision-making and planning. The SWOT Analysis provides a framework for identifying strengths, weaknesses, opportunities, and threats in a given situation, while the OODA Loop provides a framework for decision-making and action that involves four stages: observe, orient, decide, and act.

By applying the SWOT Analysis within the OODA Loop framework, individuals or businesses can use the information gathered in the observation and orientation stages to inform their decisions and actions. For example, after identifying strengths and weaknesses through the SWOT Analysis, an individual can orient themselves to the situation by analyzing how these strengths and weaknesses might impact their decision-making process. They can then use this information to make informed decisions and take appropriate actions.

Additionally, the OODA Loop can help individuals or businesses act quickly and effectively in response to identified threats and opportunities. For example, if a business identifies an opportunity through the SWOT Analysis, they can use the OODA Loop to quickly decide on a course of action and take steps to capitalize on the opportunity before it disappears.

Combining the SWOT Analysis and the OODA Loop can also be beneficial in decision-making and strategic planning. The SWOT Analysis can be used in the "observe" stage of the OODA Loop to identify the strengths, weaknesses, opportunities, and threats in a given situation or context. This information can then be used in the "orient" stage to analyze the situation and make an informed decision. The decision can then be put into action in the "decide" and "act" stages, which can be monitored and adjusted using the OODA Loop framework.

For example, a company that is considering expanding into a new market can use the SWOT Analysis to identify potential opportunities and threats in the market. The OODA Loop can then be used to analyze the situation and make a decision on whether or not to pursue the expansion. The decision can then be put into action using the OODA Loop framework, with the progress and results of the expansion being monitored and adjusted as needed.

Overall, combining different frameworks can provide a more comprehensive approach to decision-making and goal-setting, ultimately leading to more effective and efficient outcomes. By understanding the strengths and weaknesses of each framework and how they can complement each other, individuals and organizations can achieve greater success in achieving their goals and making informed decisions.

combining multiple frameworks can be a powerful way to improve productivity, achieve better results, and promote personal and professional growth. By using the strengths of each framework and applying them to different situations, individuals can effectively manage tasks, set and achieve goals, make informed decisions, and improve their overall performance. It is important to note that not every framework will work for every individual or situation, and it may take some experimentation to find the right combination. However, by taking a holistic approach and using a combination of frameworks, individuals can set themselves up for success and achieve their full potential.

This book is dedicated to my learnings and development throughout my personal life, career and self development journey, these are the frameworks and methodologies that I apply to my every day life and the processes and mindsets that I attribute to my success and personal growth.

None of this would have been possible without my peers, mentors and continuous support from those around me.

SMART GOALS

S SPECIFIC

M MEASURABLE

A ACHIEVABLE

R RELEVANT

T TIME BOUND

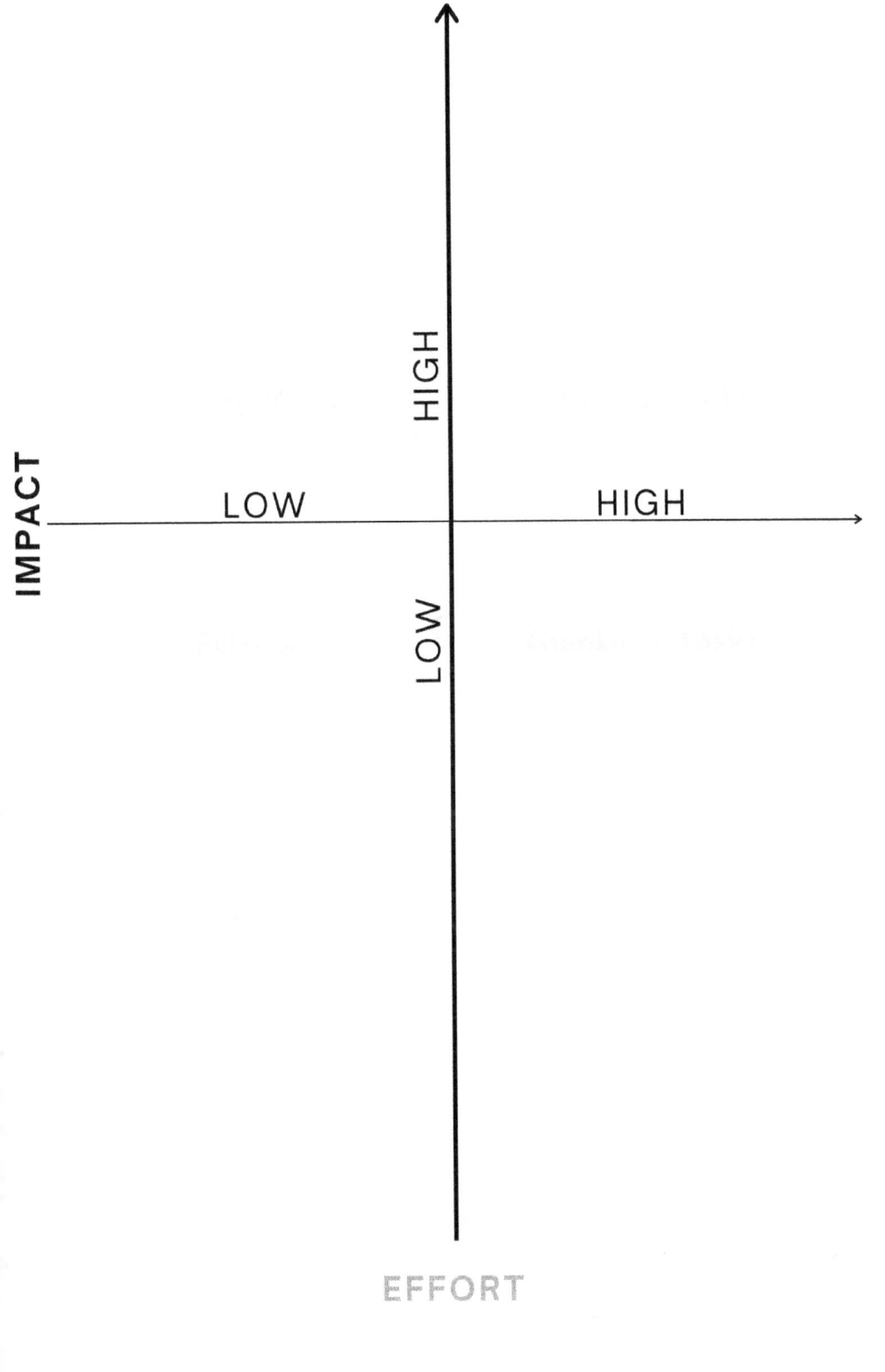

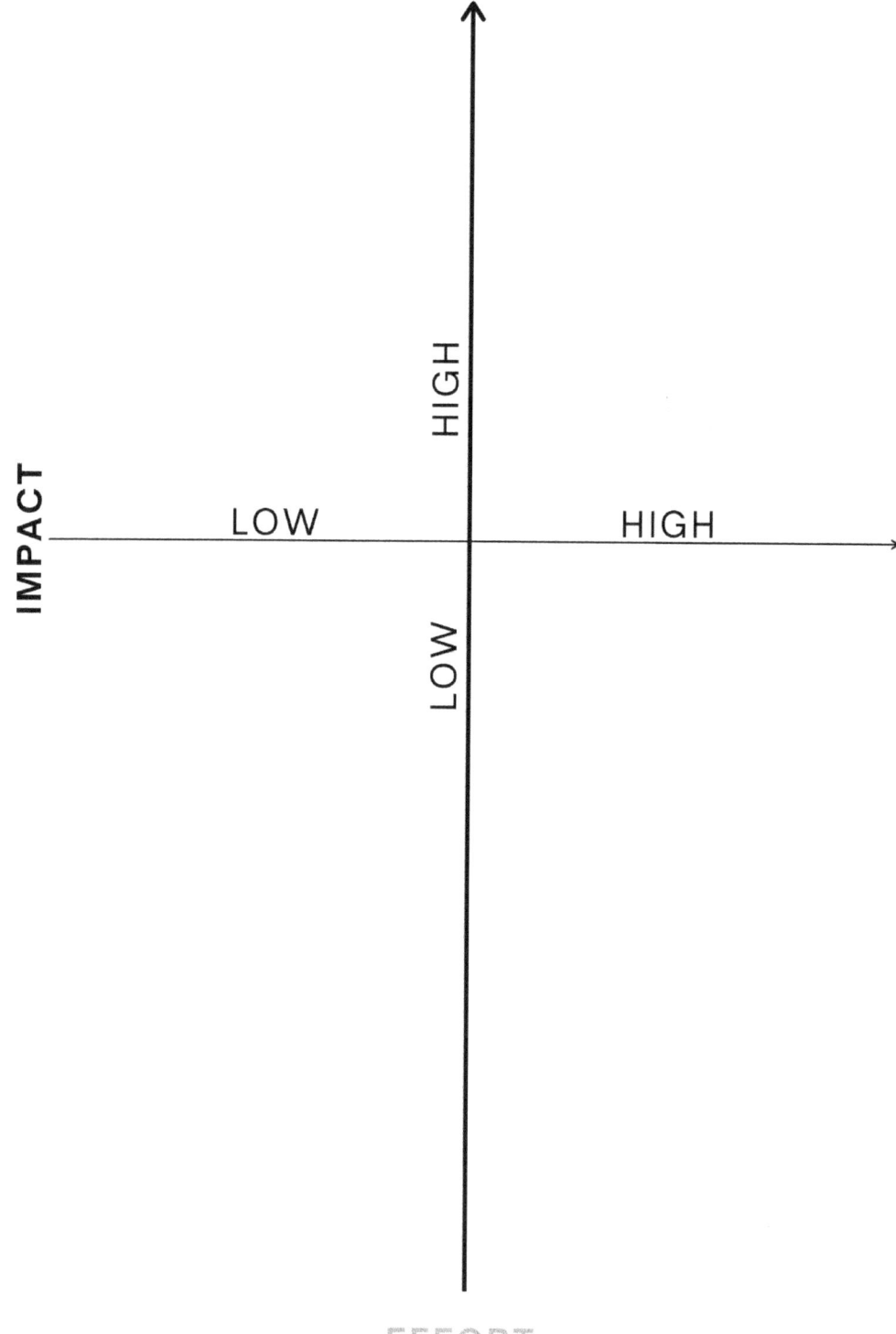

SWOT ANALYSIS

STRENGTHS	WEAKNESS

OPPORTUNITIES	THREATS

SWOT ANALYSIS

STRENGTHS	WEAKNESS

OPPORTUNITIES	THREATS